A Place of Rest
for Our
Gallant
Boys

The U.S. Army General Hospital
at Gallipolis, Ohio | 1861-1865

Christy Perry Tuohey

ISBN-13: 978-1-7378575-3-2
ISBN-10: 1-7378575-3-7

Library of Congress Control Number: 2022930109

35th Star Publishing
Charleston, West Virginia
www.35thstar.com

On the cover:
Plan of the U.S.A. General Hospital at Gallipolis, Ohio. Courtesy Massachusetts Historical Society.

Surgeon Lincoln R. Stone, 2nd & 54th Massachusetts Infantry, Surgeon-in-charge USAGH, Gallipolis, Ohio. Image courtesy John Appleton Collection, West Virginia and Regional History Center, West Virginia University.

Hannah Utley Maxon. Gallipolis teacher, U.S. Army nurse. *Program, 44th National Encampment, Grand Army of the Republic, Atlantic City, New Jersey, September 19–24, 1910.*

Corporal Joseph R. Lunbeck, Hospital Steward. Image courtesy of Gallia County Historical Society.

Cover and interior design by Studio 6 Sense

A Place of Rest
for Our
Gallant Boys

The U.S. Army General Hospital
at Gallipolis, Ohio | 1861-1865

Christy Perry Tuohey

35th Star Publishing
Charleston, West Virginia
www.35thstar.com

DEDICATION

This book is dedicated to those citizens who worked
tirelessly and relentlessly to save lives during the
United States of America's bloodiest and most divisive war.
May their descendants learn of their incredible
sacrifices and be proud of their courage.

☞ From a personal examination of the Hospital at Gallipolis, we feel justified in saying that in every respect, it is as near perfection as can be found anywhere. Few, if any hospitals in the country can compare with it. The buildings are new, large, airy, well ventilated, and in the highest possible state of cleanliness and comfort. Surely our brave soldiers who are wounded or taken sick and have the good fortune to be placed in this Hospital, should not complain. They do not, and the only difficulty is to get them away from it when fit for duty. Our farmers when they come to town, should not fail to visit the grounds and see the capital arrangement of the whole.

To Capt. Moulton too much credit cannot be given for his energy and skill in the construction of the whole, and indeed, it does honor to all concerned. As a place of rest for our gallant boys on their passing to and from home to their army, it is of immense value.— Surgeon Bell and his Assistant, spare no pains to render the inmates comfortable and happy. Unless we are much mistaken, the soldiers who have been in it, will look back with pleasure to the days they spent therein, and pray for blessings on those who so kindly ministered to their wants.

"As a place of rest for our gallant boys
on their passing to and from home to their army,
it is of immense value.

Gallipolis Journal, August 7, 1862

TABLE OF CONTENTS

Illustrations

ACKNOWLEDGMENTS

I am grateful to some Gallia County, Ohio folks without whose help I could not have written this book. Thanks to:

» Cheryl Enyart, Director of the Gallia County Historical Society
» Randall Fulks, Reference Services Manager, Dr. Samuel L. Bossard Memorial Library, Gallipolis
» Everyone who transcribes, maintains, and posts on the Gallia County Genealogical Society website and Facebook page

On the West Virginia side of the Ohio River, my thanks to Terry Lowry, retired staff historian of the West Virginia Department of Arts, Culture and History in Charleston. Also, many thanks to Steve Cunningham of 35th Star Publishing, whose personal Civil War Union Army document collections helped me in the search for USAGH Gallipolis patients.

I am also grateful to the staff of the U.S. Army Medical Library at the National Library of Medicine, Bethesda, MD, and to Archivist John Deeben at the National Archives and Records Administration, Washington, D.C.

Special thanks to Author/Blogger/Genealogist Cathy Meder-Dempsey for information on her 2nd great-grandfather Private Alexander Clonch, Company C, 13th West Virginia Infantry, who was a patient at the U.S. Army General Hospital Gallipolis, and for permission to use his photo. Thanks also to Linda Young, who gave me permission to use an image of her 2nd great-grandfather, USAGH Hospital Steward Joseph Ross Lunbeck. Nicole Hixon was also a tremendous help, providing information about and an image of her 3rd great-grandfather, Surgeon Francis Salter.

INTRODUCTION

Gallipolis, Ohio, was uniquely situated, both geographically and commercially, to become the site of one of 204 Union Army hospitals. Its location on the Ohio River, proximity to the earliest Civil War battle sites in western Virginia and well-supplied military depot made it an ideal spot to construct a hospital that could take in patients arriving via steamboat from field and post hospitals.[1] At the very outset of fighting, and before they built the General Hospital, the town gave up an elementary school and at least two other buildings to be used as hospital facilities. Post surgeons dealt with a summer of 1861 onslaught of casualties that only increased as steamer after steamer flowed down Virginia rivers and into the Ohio.

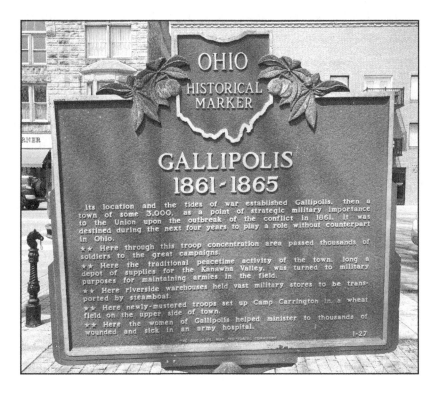

The story of the Gallipolis United States Army General Hospital started with research into my Virginia/West Virginia ancestors. Several of them fled during the war to Gallia County from western Virginia. I first became fascinated by the doctors, nurses and other staff members who worked at Gallipolis—tireless, dedicated people who worked without benefit of antibiotics or other modern medicines or surgical tools. The recent college graduate in her first teaching job who left the classroom for the sick ward. The New England surgeon who had survived Confederate capture and later treated soldiers of the 54th Massachusetts Infantry, one of the first regiments that recruited and enlisted black soldiers. The physician who performed the war's first amputation and helped save lives at the post hospital.

Then the soldiers' stories came into focus. Union and Confederate troops alike poured into town. I identified nearly 900 Union and 26 Confederate patients who were treated and/or discharged for disability from the U.S. Army General Hospital at Gallipolis. Their stories include an 11-year-old drummer boy whose instrument was shot out of his hands; a private who lost a leg in battle who asked to be transferred to Gallipolis to be close to his friends; a Confederate captain at turns lambasted by the hospital matron and asked to take tea and toast with her behind the surgeon's back; and a patient who got drunk in town and murdered a policeman as he sat in a shop doorway.

It was my goal to portray these lives in the most accurate way possible while sticking to a nonfiction narrative. Thanks to increasing digitization of military records and books and the genealogical contributions of descendants, I found many details about the people who worked at and were treated in the United States Army Hospital at Gallipolis, a riverside hospital campus that no longer exists; a simple historical marker is the only witness to the "place of rest for our gallant boys."

Chapter One

DRUMBEATS OF WAR

"Tis a busy world; see the soldier stand,
While bullets round him fall on every hand,
And with great boldness men shoot down,
While others his name with glory crown."

—W.P. Jackson, written at the U.S.A.
General Hospital, Gallipolis, OH, 1861

Fall 1860
A young teacher begins her career

Nineteen-year-old Hannah Maxon had just graduated from Springfield (Ohio) Female College when she accepted a teaching job at Union School, in her hometown of Gallipolis, Ohio.[2] She left Springfield and moved back to her childhood home.

Hannah's father, Samuel, provided his family with a comfortable living and paid for his children's education by dint of his real estate acumen and success with farming. He owned several lots in town and dozens of acres at his farm just north of Gallipolis. His property holdings were at one point valued at $12,000, equal to nearly $400,000 in today's cash. In 1850, Samuel and his wife Eliza had four children under their roof, plus a black servant and a white farmhand.[3]

Hannah was born at home and grew up in the same house on Second Avenue, along with her half-sister, seven years older, and younger brother. Their house was just a short walk away from the Ohio River. In the backyard was a pilot house, taken from the steamboat *William Phillips,* and given by the boat's captain to the children to use as a playhouse.[4]

Hannah may have still felt like a schoolgirl when she first began teaching students not much younger than herself. An excerpt from "Papers for Young Schoolmistresses," published in the 1860 *Ohio Education Monthly,* described the adjustment for first-time teachers: "You are now beholding the reality of what you have often pictured—yourself seated in a schoolroom, surrounded by the young, no longer mates, but pupils; teaching is no more an undefined, ideal event of the future—it is becoming a serious, everyday matter of fact."[5]

It is likely, though, that Hannah matured more quickly than her peers. Her father died when she was only 12. Samuel Maxon's death left the family without a steady source of income. Her mother, Eliza, had to sell all the farm tools, buggies, horses and cows. Hannah no doubt felt a great responsibility to secure a job quickly after graduating.

During the spring semester of Hannah's second year of teaching, rebel forces attacked a Union fort in South Carolina. Four slaveholding states had broken away from the Union, and the rebellion quickly turned violent. President Abraham Lincoln immediately issued a call for 75,000 volunteers to enlist and protect the remaining Union states. Hannah watched militia men drill on Public Square and read in the newspaper about Ohio soldiers heading to western Virginia. One by one, Virginia steamers docked at the town wharf, and stretcher after stretcher of bandaged troops was hauled off the ships and onto waiting hospital wagons in Gallipolis.

She heard the rumors, too, about how the houses used as an Army Post Hospital in town were hot, stuffy, and cramped. The U.S. surgeons operating there needed better facilities and had asked the city school board if Union School could be used as a hospital. She wondered where her pupils would go and how they would be educated if their classrooms were turned into sick wards. And where would she work once that happened?

May 1861

A New England doctor enlists

After graduating from Harvard Medical School, Lincoln Ripley Stone, M.D., set up a small practice in Salem, Massachusetts.[6] He may well have expected to spend his career as a town doctor, but like Hannah, he observed the rebellion stirring in the South and concluded it would not end quietly. On May 25th, 1861, a little more than a month after the attack on Fort Sumter, Dr. Stone traveled the 20-plus miles to Boston and signed up with the 2nd Massachusetts Infantry. He enlisted as the regiment's Assistant Surgeon.[7]

President Lincoln's call for volunteers led to the creation of state regiments, numbering about 1,000 men each. Each regiment had a Surgeon and an Assistant Surgeon. The Union army medical system got off to a somewhat chaotic start, with illness and injury reports coming into the Surgeon General's Office in Washington inconsistently and riddled with mistakes.

According to *The Medical and Surgical History of the War of the Rebellion,* "The necessity for a thorough revision of the Returns of Sick and Wounded becoming apparent, a Medical Board was assembled for this purpose." By July 1862, it issued the following order:

> "Medical Directors of Armies in the field will forward, direct to the Surgeon General, at Washington, duplicates of their reports to their several Commanding Generals, of the killed and wounded, after every engagement."
>
> > By order of the Secretary of War,
> > Signed,
> > E.D. Townsend, Assistant Adjutant General"[8]

Thus began a trickle of a paper trail that grew to a flood flowing from battlefields and hospitals to the nation's capital. Surgeon Stone became all too familiar with writing reports and all the ink stains and writer's cramp that came with it. It was a skill that would serve him well later in his job as a U.S. Army General Hospital administrator. But before that appointment, he would treat hundreds of soldiers in the field, even while a prisoner of war.

May 1861

A compassionate surgeon turns a courthouse into a hospital

Meanwhile, in Virginia, Surgeon Jonas Frank Gabriel of Piqua, Ohio, was patching up wounded soldiers as they came off the battlefields. Gabriel and another surgeon of the 11th Ohio Volunteer Infantry secured a courthouse to use as a makeshift hospital after a skirmish in Princeton, Virginia.

Regimental Chaplain W.W. Lyle described the scene: "The courthouse, which had been occupied as company headquarters, was cleaned out most thoroughly.

Bunks or cots were made of all the available lumber, which, at the best, was only the rough fencing boards about the town; and as much straw as could be collected within several miles was used in making the rough bunks a little more comfortable."[9]

In his Civil War memoir, Rev. Lyle noted that Dr. Gabriel was skilled, kind, and compassionate. The pastor recalled a time when the surgeon delivered the harsh news to a young, wounded soldier that he would need to undergo an amputation. "Dr. Gabriel pressed his hand warmly and spoke to him as tenderly as if he were his own brother. That little episode, at the side of that hard, rough cot, in the midst of all that was heart-rending of suffering and death, revealed to me the fact that, under all that was quiet, cool, and decided of medical skill, there could beat one of the warmest and tenderest of hearts."[10]

It may have been Dr. Gabriel's reputation that impressed the Northern Department medical director. He appointed him to be the first Post Surgeon in Charge at Gallipolis.[11]

August 1861

Three comrades and a western Virginia rout

The first land battle of the Civil War was fought at Philippi, Virginia, on June 3, 1861. Dr. James Robison of the 16th Ohio Infantry was at Philippi, and there performed the first known limb amputation of the war on a Confederate soldier named James E. Hanger.[12] Hanger would later invent and patent an artificial limb.[13] Robison would soon report for duty at Gallipolis.[14]

At Camp Dennison near Cincinnati, enlisted men of the 7th Ohio Volunteer Infantry packed their gear and headed for the Virginia hills on Wednesday evening, June 26th. They took the Central Ohio Railroad to Bellaire, Ohio, and from there were ferried across the Ohio to Benwood, about four miles below Wheeling, Virginia.[15]

After arriving at Grafton, Virginia in June, some members of the 7th who were by trade printers set up shop in an abandoned newspaper office and published a broadsheet they titled *The Ohio Seventh*. They directed a statement of purpose to the people of the region:

> "What we wish in coming here as soldiers we desire to answer. While
> in the pursuits of peace at homes that are dear to us, we heard
> that unscrupulous politicians were attempting to overthrow this

Government, and that men here who dared to plead a word in its defense were put down by lawless violence. We came to rescue our Government and its friends from ruin. Our respect for loyal men in Western Virginia has always been great, and we assure you that it has not decreased since we came among you. All we desire is to establish the authority of the Government and to strengthen your hands in its defense. This accomplished and we will return to our homes, leaving you in the full enjoyment of all your rights as you have enjoyed them since the foundation of the Government. Can you ask more?"[16]

By mid-August, Company C of the 7th OVI was stationed in Nicholas County, Virginia, an area nearly deserted after Rebel sympathizers fled. Many Union men were also leaving. On August 8th, the Confederate congress passed the Alien Enemies Act, which required all males fourteen years old and older living in slave states to sign the Confederate oath or leave the state within 40 days. The penalty: arrest and probable imprisonment.[17]

Company C Private Leroy Warren wrote in his diary about what happened in late August at the Battle of Kessler's Cross Lanes, near Summersville, Virginia.

"Little did I know Sunday night what the morrow was to bring forth."

"We got up about daylight and began to shake and warm ourselves. We fell upon four beeves [cattle] which the Confederates had slaughtered the day before for their own use. Two or three wagons of our train came up with hard bread and we procured green corn from the fields."

"While we were still breakfasting we heard the rapid firing to the south. We seized our muskets and formed Company. The Colonel [Erastus B. Tyler] was among us. He ordered our Company and Company A to occupy a hill to the southwest of the corners. We double-quicked a few rods down to the south road and then turned to the right over the fence."

"But before we left the road, we were fired upon in front—and in flank by a line of men—who suddenly appeared on the brow of a hill east of the road and within good musket range. We still had two fields to cross—a fence and a hill to climb—before we could get to the position we had been ordered to occupy. We ran like a flock of frightened deer across the fields, over the fence and up the hill—subject, all this while, to fire which we could not return."

"The bullets whistled all around us. They fell like thickest hail. It seems that no more of our men were wounded at this time—but we were very much scattered and running with all our might—so that it must been difficult to take aim at us. Three or four of our Company there were wounded—one perhaps fatally."[18]

Soldiers scattered, crashing through corn stalks and up the side of a mountain, crawling through thickets and underbrush. Private Edgar Condit picks up the story from there:

"Immediately following the battle, Company C hurriedly left the field, taking to the nearby woods, in a more or less demoralized condition. However, our real confusion and flight followed several hours later, when we suddenly found ourselves almost entirely surrounded by [Confederate] Colonel Tompkins's regiment. The first we knew of their presence was their demand for our surrender. This happened at a time when most of the company were sitting on the ground resting, while the Captain and some of the sergeants had begun a conference as to the direction we should take. The enemy had also been resting, but quickly rising up, their guns were fairly in our faces. In a sorrowful tone of voice Captain Shurtleff gave the order, 'Fall in, boys, I shall have to give you up.'"[19]

Condit escaped, but 38 men were captured and forced on a long march to Richmond, Virginia. Three others from Company C escaped as well: Private James R. Bell, M.D., the regiment's hospital steward; Private Charles C. Bosworth, a regimental nurse; and Surgeon Francis Salter, the assistant surgeon of the 7th.

First Lieutenant William D. Shepherd of Company D recalled that some got away more quickly than others who hid on the mountain: "Colonels Tyler and Creighton, Surgeon Salter and Chaplain Brown now dashed up the Gauley Road and made their escape to the bridge. The retreat of the Seventh, which occupied three and one-half days (from Monday at sunrise until Thursday noon), was perhaps and ever will be the greatest event in the lives of many if not all engaged in it."

When the rest of the regiment finally reunited and traveled to Charleston, Virginia, the paths of Privates Bell and Bosworth and Surgeon Salter would intersect again. The three would end up at a Virginia Post hospital, one of them gravely ill.

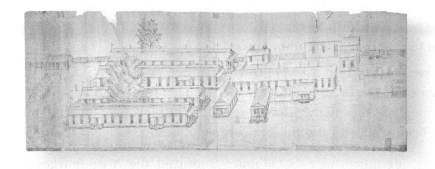

Chapter Two

THE ROCKY ROAD TO THE HOSPITAL

"At present the health of the regiment is not
a good as it commonly is, for the men are worn
out by forced marches and exposure; the measles are
raging to some extent here just now..."

—Letter from a soldier of the 36th Regiment, Ohio Volunteer Infantry
stationed in Summersville, VA, to the *Gallipolis Journal*, November 14, 1861.

Back in Gallipolis, sick and wounded soldiers packed onto ambulances wagons and shipped down to the Kanawha River – and on to the Ohio - were arriving in increasingly large numbers. The town was a major supply depot even before the war broke out and was well-located as a stopping point for the flow of casualties.

The wounded first had to survive the journey. Often, the rough road from battle-field to hospital itself caused injuries. A special war correspondent to the *New York Herald* sent eyewitness accounts from Virginia to *The New York Tribune*:

"Since I have been with the army, I have frequently been astounded at the removal of badly wounded patients from the field hospitals to the base hospitals, over roads that it would almost take the life of a well man to ride over in an ambulance."

"I have thought that if I were thus wounded I would rather take my chances on the field, without medical aid, in the rain and sun, and at the mercy of the enemy, than to be thus murderously tortured after I had been rescued from the fiery ordeal of battle."[20]

The writer, identified only as "Illinoien," praised the Army surgeons who out-fitted their Virginia field hospital more efficiently than others he had seen. He mentioned Dr. C.A. Barlow, Surgeon of the 62nd Ohio, for innovating a safer, cleaner type of field hospital where the wounded could be kept for longer peri-ods of time and perhaps not transported to base hospitals at all. Dr. Charles Augustus Barlow (also known as Augustus Charles) was a local physician from Gallipolis, who had also served in the 8th [West] Virginia Infantry as well as the 47th Ohio Infantry.

The wounded patients who survived the trip presented surgeons with tough choices. 11th Ohio Infantry Surgeon J. Frank Gabriel, who had been transferred from the Kanawha Valley, Virginia District Post Hospital to Gallipolis, examined one soldier whose thigh had been crushed by cannon shot. He considered per-forming a hip-joint amputation on the young man but decided against it because the soldier was not likely to survive.[21]

A greater number of early war victims succumbed to diseases like typhoid fever, measles, pneumonia and dysentery than to injuries. One was 28-year-old Private William Honeywell of Ohio's 21st Infantry, who died of pneumonia at the Gallipolis Post hospital on July 4, 1861. A fellow soldier, identified only by his initials "D.H.P.", wrote a poem in tribute to Honeywell, published in the *Gallipolis Journal.* An excerpt:

> His Country's call he did obey,
>
> And died from home, far, far away,
>
> And though no foe his blood did stain,
>
> On traitor's heads it will remain.
>
> Comrade rest, life's battle's o'er,
>
> Sweetly sleep on Freedom's shore
>
> Till the trump with awful sound,
>
> Wakes the sleepers underground.[22]

The town newspaper was replete with war information. Editor James Harper frequently ran local soldiers' letters penned from wherever they were stationed. There were also thank-you letters from Army hospital patients. One, titled "Letter from a Sick Soldier," was especially grateful to local ladies who brought food and other supplies to the hospital.

"....for truly, it seems like a home here, when we see kind-hearted, benevolent ladies, administering so attentively to the wants of the sick and wounded, from day to day. It is cheering to the heart of a sick soldier to know and feel that there is someone who takes an interest in his welfare, in administering to his wants, while he is sick and far from the loved ones at home. And how cheering it must be to our friends and relations to know that here in Gallipolis, sick and wounded, we are well cared for. That there are kind hands to cool the fevered brows of their sons and husbands, to furnish those little nourishing delicacies which cannot be expected from an army hospital, only through the benevolence of kind hearts. Ladies of Gallipolis, we can never repay you for your trouble."[23]

Surgeon Francis Salter was placed in charge of the Charleston post hospital. Salter, who had been born and raised in England and emigrated to the United States in the 1850s, had established a medical practice in Circleville. About a month after the war began, he was recommended for service as an Army surgeon. His 7th Ohio comrades Dr. James Bell and Charles Bosworth were assigned to work with Salter at Charleston, as hospital steward and nurse, respectively.

While at Charleston, Bell's health took a serious turn. While on duty in September, he experienced a sharp pain in his left eye. Twenty-four hours later the pain filled his entire body, most severely in his left leg and hip. By the third day of the attack, he could not move and required two nurses to monitor and care for him. Bosworth was one of Bell's nurses and recalled that Bell "was suddenly prostrated by an attack of neuralgia and was confined to his bed for a period of ten days, and he was pronounced by Surgeon Salter to be in a very dangerous condition."[24]

Despite the serious health scare, Bell did gradually recover. By the time he had, Dr. Salter was ordered to Gallipolis to be post surgeon. Both Bell and Bosworth would also end up in Gallipolis.

In returning to Ohio to work at the Gallipolis post, Dr. Salter was at least closer to his family. He and his wife Mary Jane, both UK natives, had five children, and the family lived in Noble County, Ohio.[25] The older three boys were born in England, a fourth in New York, and baby Mary was born in Ohio.

A photo of him in his dress surgeon's uniform, including sword and sheath, shows he had dark hair, curly tufts sneaking out below his kepi, and a goatee.

Assistant Surgeon Francis Salter
Photo courtesy of Salter descendant Nicole Hixon

On September 29, 1861, a representative of the U.S. Sanitary Commission, an organization created by relief agency volunteers who aided the government in providing sanitary conditions and medical supplies to the emerging war hospitals, inspected the Gallipolis houses being used as hospital wards.

Wheeling, Virginia Doctor C.D. Griswold conducted the September Gallipolis inspection. He met with Surgeon Gabriel and found that there were 129 sick in what he described as two small, ill-constructed houses with small rooms and mostly immovable windows, "which made proper ventilation impossible." Hospital stores, medicines and instruments were inadequate, he wrote, and a village pharmacist provided all drugs.[26]

Dr. Griswold's report warned that Gallipolis needed bigger, better medical accommodations, but it would take four to six weeks to build hospital barracks. He concluded that the Union School was the only building in town suitable for hospital use. Based on his recommendations, the U.S. Army Medical Department called upon the school board to consent to hosting an Army hospital. The Board agreed.

Hannah Maxon made up her mind. If she could not teach at Union School, she would serve there as a Union nurse.

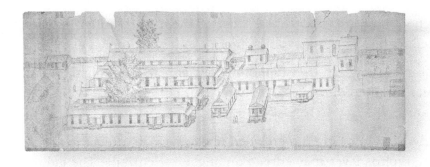

Chapter Three

FROM SCHOOLROOMS TO SICK WARDS

*"We have to stand guard here every night on the border, from Gallipolis to
Guyandotte, as there are rumors that [Confederate Generals] Wise and Jenkins
intend to cross over and attack us. We are determined to defend ourselves to the
last extremity. The women stay up all night and sleep all day, and the men
have provided a place of safety for them in case of attack."*

—"Stirring Times on the Ohio Border,"
The New York Times, Sunday, July 21, 1861[27]

F ear mounted among citizens living on both sides of the Ohio River, as word
spread that Confederate General Henry Wise was encamped at Charleston,
Virginia, about sixty miles southeast of Gallipolis. Gallipolis was a small yet
important depot serving the U.S. Army's Northern Department. A Rebel attack on
the ammunition and provisions stored in the town's warehouses could seriously
disable the Union effort in that region.

Constant, cold autumn rains in the Ohio Valley region swelled river levels. The
damp, clammy mountains of western Virginia became viral and bacterial jungles.
Hundreds of soldiers serving there fell sick from exposure and extreme fatigue.
Over 400 soldiers from General Rosecrans' and Cox's forces were brought to the

Union School hospital in October. Most of them were suffering with what they then called "camp fever," or typhus, more commonly known as typhoid fever.

There was great concern that typhoid might spread from hospital patients to the community at large. James Harper wrote an editorial that addressed residents' growing anxiety.

"... the hospitals here are crowded to excess, and unless great care is taken, typhus fever may spread amongst our citizens. The ladies of Gallipolis with that sympathy for suffering humanity, for which they are proverbial, crowd to the hospital to render any assistance possible to the men, regardless of their own danger. The spirit in which it is done is commendable. The policy of it is doubtful. The hospitals we know are poorly furnished with nurses or cooks. The physicians are doing their utmost, but what can two men, skillful as they are, effect among so many? Government ought at once to provide nurses and cooks, plenty of whom can be hired in town, poor persons who would be glad to earn a living by it."[28]

Harper may have referred to hospitals, plural, because besides the Post Hospital, The First Presbyterian Church's Lyceum Hall was being used "for hospital purposes." There is evidence that a Point Pleasant, Virginia, inn just across the Ohio River housed troops for a few months. A news item in a late February *Gallipolis Journal* stated that, "The occupation of the Kline House in Point Pleasant, as a hospital, may serve to relieve us of the sick in the Union School House and afford the teachers a chance for a livelihood as well as the children, a refuge from the dangers that surround them on the streets. We are not complaining of the military authorities, for thus occupying our public buildings, but merely state facts in order to call the attention of parents to the responsibility resting upon them in regard to the education of their children."[29]

The two surgeons in charge at that point were J. Frank Gabriel and James Dickey Robison, of first Civil War amputation fame. They had western Virginia combat duty in common. Robison had been attached to General William Rosecrans' Army of Occupation and was on the scene at the September 10th Battle of Carnifex Ferry. Carnifex was the second Nicholas County, Virginia, skirmish, fought fifteen days after the Battle of Kesslers Cross Lanes, from which Salter, Bell and Bosworth had escaped.

James Dickey Robison, M.D. *Commemorative biographical record
of Wayne County, Ohio, containing biographical sketches of prominent
and representative citizens, and of many of the early settled families.*

Drs. Robison and Gabriel set about reorganizing at the post hospital. As the
saying goes, however, no good deed goes unpunished. *Journal* Editor Harper
was hearing complaints from citizens who had provided supplies or labor to the
hospital.

> "It seems that Dr. J.F. Gabriel made no return of the number of sick
> to the Commissary, so as to draw rations to constitute a hospital
> fund. That is the only obstacle in the way and if it were done yet, the
> Commissary is willing and anxious to pay the debts contracted by
> Dr. Gabriel. It is to be hoped the Dr., whom we have always highly
> esteemed, will without delay, make out the rolls, so that payment may
> be made."[30]

By the editor's own admission, though, there was only a skeleton hospital staff.
Drs. Robison and Gabriel, joined by Dr. Salter in mid-October, treated all patients.
It is easy to conclude that Surgeon Gabriel, lauded for his tender care of wounded

soldiers on the battlefield, may have had neither the time nor administrative skills necessary to expedite paperwork and payrolls while receiving mounting boatloads of casualties.

It quickly became apparent that the primary work of a Surgeon in Charge of such a facility was to spend hours signing letters and documents at a desk rather than sewing up incisions in an operating room. Surgeon Gabriel's administrative duties at Gallipolis did not last long. In early December 1861, he rejoined his regiment when they went into winter quarters at Point Pleasant. He remained with them until health problems forced him to resign in the fall of 1862.

By the start of the elementary school fall term, Union School had fully transformed into a hospital. Gallipolis women outfitted school rooms with several hundred beds lined up beneath blackboards. For the time being, it forced students to attend classes in the basements of the Baptist and Methodist Churches.

Hannah joined many other women in the city in delivering food and other aid to the school. Soon enough, she was nursing patients there. Though she was not medically trained, she applied for a position and followed U.S. Army rules and regulations. Records show that she enlisted as a nurse in the Medical Department, U.S. Volunteers, on October 10, 1861.[31]

That Hannah, trained as a teacher, could become a nurse was not all that unusual at the time. No formal nursing schools existed in the U.S. when the Civil War broke out. Most medical personnel learned their healing skills on the job from medical school-educated surgeons. At that point in the nineteenth century, laws governing physicians were not rigorous, and earning a medical degree was somewhat easy, after one served an apprenticeship and took a few courses at a medical college. In one unusual case, an Ohio marble cutter and sculptor became a veterinary surgeon with the 1st West Virginia Cavalry.

The Army categorized hospital attendants as follows: enlisted men, the hospital corps (civilians employed as cooks and nurses at General Hospitals), and female nurses. At the beginning of the war, all personnel were white people. The first official Army hospital nurses were enlisted men, but in the months after combat began, women across the country were volunteering, some who were wives, sisters, mothers and other relatives of soldiers.

Although female nurses could not live in military camps along with soldiers and officers or accompany them on marches, they were considered for hospital work. Dorothea Dix, a social reformer who was named Superintendent of the United States Army Nurses, hired a corps of women nurses. Dix herself did not have medical training, but she was said to have "extraordinary organizational skills," had worked for mental health care reform in the U.S., and had become adept at navigating social and political systems. Dix required strong references for her job candidates. According to *The Army Surgeon's Manual*, "All applicants must present certificates of qualification and good character from at least two persons of trust, testifying to morality, integrity, seriousness, and capacity for care of the sick."[32]

Hannah Utley Maxon. Gallipolis teacher, U.S. Army nurse.
Program, Forty Fourth National Encampment, Grand Army of the Republic,
Atlantic City, New Jersey, September 19-24, 1910

Hannah was appointed to Dix's corps of army nurses, and she served with distinction throughout the entire war.[33] Her maturity likely made her a good fit for Army nursing. It was later said of her Army nurse work, "Bringing into her work, as she did, youth, courage, strength and unselfish devotion to the cause she thought was right, Miss Maxon made a most capable and efficient nurse."[34]

The rules for nurses under Dix's leadership were strict and clear cut. "Matronly persons of experience, good conduct, or superior education and serious disposition will always have preference; habits of neatness, order, sobriety, and industry are prerequisites."

At 21 years old, being young and strong no doubt helped Hannah carry out nursing duties. The Army wanted "only women of strong health, not subjects of chronic disease, nor liable to sudden illnesses... the duties of the station make large and continued demands on strength." According to Education Coordinator of the National Museum of Civil War Medicine John Lustrea, Civil War nurses had to prove that they had immunity from smallpox and measles.[35]

If she had any tendency toward wearing jewelry or lace, Hannah could not have worn them on duty. Army nurses were instructed to wear only solid brown, grey, or black dresses, "without ornaments of any sort," "with no bows, no curls, or jewelry, and no hoop skirts." Her work uniform was plain, her hair swept up into her signature topknot. According to Lustrea, under nineteenth century Victorian mores, any hint of romance or sexual impropriety that might have arisen from placing females in close contact with males in the military was strongly discouraged.

As part of the Hospital Corps team, Hannah reported to Surgeon Gabriel. The men who worked as nurses or cooks received $20.50 per month—roughly 68 cents per day—besides one food ration daily and the same allowance of clothing as a private infantry soldier.

In 1861, female nurses were unpaid and had to cover their own expenses. Hannah would have worked her first three years at Union School and the U.S. Army Hospital for free and relied on her family for room, board, food, etc. Others remembered Hannah as an energetic, enthusiastic caregiver. "Miss Maxon, by her zeal and activity, became prominent in this work, and took a leading part, and no doubt brought comfort and solace to many a weary one, who was far away from home and any soft and tender female hand to make smooth his dying pillow."[36]

Although the press criticized Dr. Gabriel's lack of administrative skill, Hannah, whose nature was to step in and help, apparently filled some of that void. She was described, later in her life, as having "rare executive ability." In the early, disorganized days of war hospitals, she kept an accurate record of every person brought to the hospital and provided the register to the U.S. government at war's end.[37]

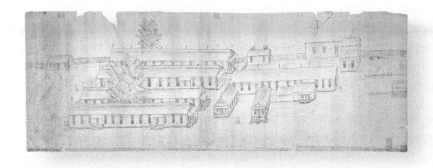

Chapter Four

GALLIPOLIS GETS A GOVERNMENT HOSPITAL

"The public schools for the fall and winter terms will commence on Monday next, and in consideration of the Union School House having been devoted to hospital purposes, the schools for the present will be held in the basements of the Baptist and Methodist Churches, and at the large frame building on the corner of Second and Grape Streets."

—*Gallipolis Journal*, October 3, 1861

When he arrived at Union School Hospital in 1862, Surgeon James Bell reunited with his 7th OVI comrade, Surgeon Salter, who had cared for him in Virginia. As Bell, Salter and Robison teamed up to treat patients at the school, plans for a new hospital were being drawn up. Post quartermasters began ordering construction supplies. A report in the *Journal* detailed the beginnings of the project:

"Capt. C.M. Moulton [depot quartermaster] has received instructions from headquarters to erect a Government Hospital at Gallipolis, as soon as practicable. This will afford employment to our mechanics, and be the means of disbursing a large sum of money, where it is most needed. The fact of this institution being located here speaks volumes in favor of the health of our town. Being easy of access from all points, the terminus of navigation on the Kanawha, together with freedom from any danger of high water, no place in the Ohio valley is so well calculated for a Hospital for the Mountain Department as Gallipolis."[38]

The large bodies of troops moving early in the war across western Virginia and the need for better hospital buildings in that region led to the creation of long, ridge-ventilated wooden sheds for hospital wards, also called pavilions. Assistant Surgeon Jonathan Letterman, known for developing and implementing the first Ambulance Corps, oversaw this effort. The roofs of such wards were vented at their ridges to allow ventilation and also some protection from inclement weather.[39] The first ridge-ventilated Army hospital barrack was built at Parkersburg, Virginia. Its dimensions were 130 x 25 x 14 feet to the eaves and partitioned into four wards containing twenty beds each.[40]

Movement of fresh air through hospital wards was of utmost importance in keeping the spread of infection down in medical settings. After her 1850s medical service in the Crimean War, Nurse Florence Nightingale researched hospitals in Europe, the UK and the Middle East to find the best possible hospital design. She emphasized the importance of air circulation in sick wards as she sought to help develop better, healthier hospital environments.

In her book, *Notes on Hospitals*, Nightingale wrote:

> "Every adult exhales by the lungs and skin forty-eight ounces, or three pints of water, in twenty-four hours. Sixteen men in a room would therefore exhale in eight hours sixteen pints of water, and 123 cubic feet of carbonic, into the atmosphere of the room. With the watery vapour there is also exhaled a large quantity of organic matter, ready to enter into the putrefactive condition."[41]

> "If this be so for the well, how much more will it be so for the sick? — for the sick, the exhalations from whom are always highly morbid and dangerous, as they are one of nature's methods of eliminating noxious matter from the body, in order that it may recover health. Indeed, this is so well acknowledged that it has given rise to all the doctrine of infection—to a just horror of breathing what comes from the sick, even to the morbid fear of entering a cabin which a case of fever or smallpox has been for half an hour."

Despite Nightingale's findings, there was concern in the military medical community that too much cold air could bring on illness. Assistant Surgeon Lewis

Eastman, who reported on the use of ridge-ventilated wards at the U.S. Army General Hospital at Grafton, Virginia, in April 1862, wrote that "It is very difficult, in ordinary buildings used as hospitals, to secure ventilation without exposing the inmates to injurious draughts of air. This difficulty is avoided in the building now being constructed in accordance with the orders of Assistant Surgeon Letterman, U.S. Army, by means of 'ridge ventilation,' which keeps the air constantly pure without exposing anyone to unpleasant or dangerous draughts."[42]

One major drawback of such hospital buildings was that they did not retain heat in cold weather. As described by Surgeon George Oliver, "The declivity of the ground causes them to stand high; the sides are of rough upright boards with crevices not battened to their full height; and the ridge ventilators having no sash or shutter to close, the cold wind and snow penetrate to an extent unbearable by the patients."[43] For this reason, Army quartermasters soon began ordering wood or coal-burning stoves for the ridge-ventilated wards.

Post Quartermaster Captain Charles Moulton oversaw a crew that began building four hospital buildings on a patch of land "with a fine view of the river." There was a gap in time, between the opening of the new Gallipolis U.S. Army General Hospital and the re-opening of Union School to pupils.

News accounts pinpoint Union School's use as a hospital from October 1861 to the first week of January 1862. There was some controversy when the students returned, however. Some parents worried that insufficient cleaning of the school after soldiers had left was causing their children's winter ills. But no evidence of any connection between unclean facilities and students becoming sick surfaced.

We know that the new hospital was not finished in late May, because in the May 22nd edition of the *Gallipolis Journal,* Editor Harper advises locals applying for hospital jobs:

> "Matron—better wait until the hospital is complete and ready for soldiers. We do not know who will be placed in charge, but you might ascertain by calling on Captain Moulton, the Quartermaster at this place. Your services will doubtless be accepted and at the proper time we will present your name to the officer."[44]

Also that winter, a young soldier from Chillicothe, Ohio, Joseph Ross Lunbeck, arrived at the post hospital in Charleston, Virginia, to work as a hospital steward. Lunbeck, twenty-five years old, was a blond-haired, blue-eyed graduate of Ohio Wesleyan University, where he had been a student in the college's Scientific Department.

Corporal Joseph R. Lunbeck, Hospital Steward
Image courtesy of Gallia County Historical Society

He came to the post highly recommended. Surgeon Matthew McEwen wrote that Lunbeck "was detailed for this post, by General Rosecrans, Jan. 1st, 1862, has been constantly on duty since, and has given entire satisfaction." Department of Western Virginia Medical Director W.W. Holmes wrote on the letter "I heartily approve the above recommendation." Surgeon L.H. Holden, Medical Director of the Department of the Ohio, forwarded that recommendation to Surgeon General William A. Hammond. On January 5, 1863, Assistant Adjutant General E.D. Townsend signed Special Orders No. 5, which honorably discharged Lunbeck from service to his regiment in order to enlist as Hospital Steward, U.S. Army at Cincinnati.[45]

Thanks to his hard work and outstanding skills, Joseph Lunbeck would soon report at Gallipolis.

The First Battle of Winchester, Virginia, was fought on May 25, 1862. Seven Union doctors, including Surgeon Lincoln R. Stone of the 2nd Massachusetts, stayed at Winchester to treat the wounded after their regiments had moved on. Confederate forces took the surgeons working at a field hospital prisoner.

Confederate Medical Director Hunter Holmes McGuire, who served under General Stonewall Jackson, intervened. Doctor McGuire suggested to Jackson that the physicians be considered noncombatants and released in exchange for Rebel doctors. A Confederate naval surgeon seconded the idea, and both armies eventually changed their policies on physicians and chaplains, so that those who provided care and comfort to troops would not be captured going forward. In an exchange that came to be known as the Winchester Accord, Dr. Stone and his six fellow Union physicians were released, as were seven Confederate doctors.[46]

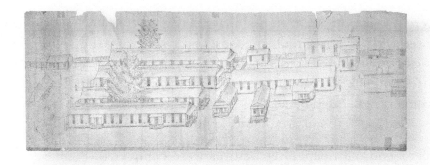

Chapter Five

AN INSIDE LOOK AT A CIVIL WAR HOSPITAL WARD

"Conflicts involving food impelled women to action more than any other cause. Surgeons regarded home-prepared foods as harmful to convalescents, but nurses who believed that they knew better insisted that patients should enjoy them." [47]

—Jane E. Schultz, *Women at the Front: Hospital Workers in Civil War America*

On May 29th, 1862, the General Hospital was progressing and one building would be ready for patients at the end of that week. On June 5th, the framework of the second ward building had gone up. "The finished building is nicely whitewashed and presents a very fine appearance," Harper wrote. "Economy in the construction, yet with an eye to the comfort of the sick has characterized the whole work, which throughout is highly creditable to all concerned."

The editor described the hospital site:

"The buildings are beautifully located on a rising ground outside of town... with a fine view of the river, where the air is always pure and free from dust. The arrangement of the buildings is most admirable as to ventilation, cleanliness and light. They are strongly built, and in every respect the 'right thing in the right place.' The whole will be enclosed with a substantial fence, and every means adopted to render the sick and wounded soldier comfortable. Indeed it already looks so cheerful and cozy, we should almost agree to be sick a short time, for the comfort of being housed therein and attended to, as we know our ladies (God bless them) are bound to do."[48]

By summer's end, all hospital structures were completed. Four were dedicated hospital wards. The fifth served as both an office and dispensary. Buildings six and seven were surgeon and staff quarters. Rounding out the buildings, which totaled fourteen, were a dining hall and kitchen, bakery, laundry and linen room, a stable, carpenter's shop, house for the dead, and a coal house.[49]

A visitor facing the new U.S. Army General Hospital would have seen the four wooden, ridge-ventilated wards to the left, lined up one behind the other. The dining room stood in the center of the campus, with the office/dispensary to the front of it, next to the staff and surgeon living quarters. Behind the dining hall were the kitchen, bakery, laundry and icehouse. Further back, the carpenter's shop, stable and dead house were on the right side of the grounds. Gardens bordered the left and rear of the wards.[50]

Each ward could hold up to fifty iron beds standing three feet apart. Army regulations provided details on how the beds should be assembled.

"The bed-furniture consists of a mattress or bedsack, sheets, blankets, a coverlet, pillow, and pillowcase. The best mattresses are undoubtedly those stuffed with hair. They are the most comfortable, the most durable, and are less liable to become impregnated with unhealthy exhalations proceeding from the patients, and thus to give rise to disease in those subsequently occupying them, than any others... special care should be used for their preservation, oiled silk or oil cloth or gutta-percha [gum tree, similar to rubber] cloth being introduced between the sheet and the mattress in all cases in which the discharge from wounds, or the probability of hemorrhage, or any other cause, renders them liable to be soiled."[51]

In the absence of mattresses, bedsacks could be used on patient beds. They were straw-filled and hospital workers could easily remove the straw, wash the covers and stuff them with new straw in between patients.

Each bed had a ticket with the patient's name, rank, regiment and company, disease or other affliction, and date of admission. On the ticket's flip side, attendants

Plan of U.S.A. Hospital, Gallipolis, Ohio, courtesy Massachusetts Historical Society.

wrote a list of the patient's personal effects. These tickets are also referred to as hospital bed cards.

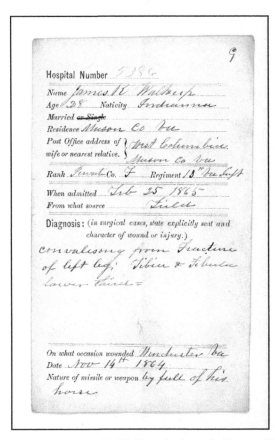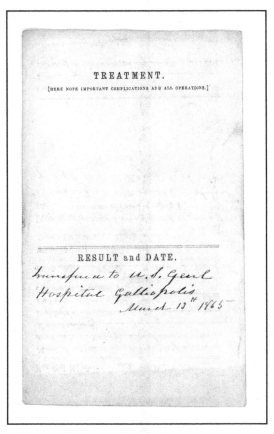

James R. Walkup bed card, Clarysville Civil War Hospital Digital Collection,
West Virginia & Regional History Center, West Virginia University,
Morgantown, West Virginia.

There was one small table or stand between each pair of beds, which held medicines and other patient items. There was also a chair for every one or two beds. Other hospital ward items included spittoons, urinals, chamber pots and chamber chairs.

Each ward had one bathroom containing cast-iron tubs. Whenever possible, both hot and cold water was made available for bathing. Separate from bathrooms were lavatories, where recovering patients and hospital attendants would wash their hands and faces. Lavatories were fitted with long tables or shelves lined with tin basins, soap and towels. Recovering patients who were able to walk to the hospital dining room for meals were required to wash their faces and hands and comb their hair before breakfast.[52]

A Surgeon in Charge headed each U.S. Army General Hospital. Surgeons of Volunteers, who ranked as majors, were the General Hospitals' senior medical officers. They supervised every facet of hospital operations, from ordering medical supplies to distributing patients into wards, where the Assistant Surgeons cared for them. The Surgeon in Charge visited patients every day, accompanied by an assistant surgeon, hospital steward, and a nurse.

Everything from patients' knapsacks to the cooks' paychecks were under the chief surgeon's purview. If a soldier left or was discharged from duty while a hospital patient, he wrote the final statements for pay and clothing and certified the soldier's descriptive lists—the written accounts of his enlistment and muster-in dates and locations, physical characteristics (height, hair and eye color, etc.), payments and stoppages and status at each muster roll call. If a patient died in the hospital, the surgeon held his personal effects until a loved one or friend might pick them up.[53]

Medical officers wore dark blue, double-breasted frock coats with buttons and shoulder straps that reflected their rank. The trousers were dark blue with thin gold cord, and medical officers' sashes were green.[54]

The steward, under the Surgeon in Charge's supervision, was the overseer for the hospital stores and supplies and issued orders to the wardmasters, cooks and nurses. The steward also distributed meals to the wards. Each hospital had at least one steward, whose rank was that of an ordnance sergeant, which meant all enlisted men in the hospital were to show the steward the military respect fitting for his position.[55]

U.S. Army General hospital stewards were required to be no younger than eighteen and no older than 35 years old. Stewards had a practical knowledge of pharmacy and were familiar with basic elements of health care including minor surgery, application of bandages and dressings, tooth extraction, and bloodletting with leeches. They were also to have a basic knowledge of cooking in order to oversee the regular hospital kitchen. Stewards were also responsible for the cleanliness of wards and kitchens, patients and attendants.

Stewards had both dress and undress uniforms, the former worn only at musters and inspections. For ordinary duties, they wore blouses or sack-coats and trousers like those of all foot soldiers. Strips of crimson lace adorned trouser seams, and the undress coat sported a half chevron. The dress uniform required a black felt hat with buff and green cords and a feather.

Wardmasters, who answered to stewards, were typically nurses. They collected a patient's belongings, recording, numbering and labeling the items in a book. Wardmasters received and distributed furniture, bedding and cooking utensils for each patient's use and kept track of whether or how they were used. They also took care of the hospital knapsack room.[56]

Nursing education being non-existent before the Civil War, caregivers experimented, tested and shared their medical and nutritional findings with others. No group did more to keep records documenting nursing work than the Women's Central Association for Relief (WCAR), "one of the earliest assistance groups founded in the North." The WCAR was organized by Dr. Elizabeth Blackwell, the first female physician in the United States, and her sister, Emily, who was the third woman in the country to earn a medical degree.[57]

The WCAR created the *Civil War Manual for Army Nurses* as a booklet distributed to all Union hospitals. It included recipes for drinks and food for the sick, types of baths recommended by doctors and solutions for gastrointestinal complaints.

Hannah and her fellow nurses might have, for example, prepared toast water for patients:

> "Cut a slice of stale bread, about twice the usual thickness; toast it carefully until thoroughly browned; put it into a quart of boiling water, and let it stand till it is quite cold; the fresher it is the better. A little currant jelly, dried orange-peel, a roasted apple, or a slice of lemon infused with the bread, are grateful additions."[58]

Some ingredients common in the nineteenth century are practically unknown to us today. There is a therapeutic beverage recipe for isinglass water, isinglass being a kind of gelatin obtained from fish. Orgeat syrup was used in making currant water for patients; a mixture of barley or almonds, sugar and rose or orange flower water created the syrup. You may know of it if you favor Mai Tais; it is still used in those cocktails today.

Nurses concocted a cold dessert known as sago posset in hospital kitchens. Its base ingredient was the pith of palm trees or other tropical plants. "Sago affords very little nourishment, and is therefore well adapted for invalids labouring under acute diseases," according to Charles Dinneford's *A Family Medicine Directory*, published in London in 1845.[59]

Government leaders encouraged farmers and gardeners to share their bounties with the military hospitals. Ohio Governor David Tod sent out a request to "The

Ladies of Ohio" to provide vegetables and fruits to the hospitals, including pickled cabbage, cucumbers, onions and apples and peaches, either canned or dried.[60] In the 1860s, fruits and vegetables were the staples of home and farm canning, but canning was not a proven method of preservation for other types of foods. The U.S. Sanitary Commission in Cincinnati asked the public in a newspaper announcement for "canned fruit, dried fruits, jellies, wines. It is hardly necessary to say that experiments in canning meats and chickens have proved a complete failure."[61]

Citizen generosity toward the early Civil War hospitals, many still set up in hotels, homes and churches at the close of the war's first year, was plentiful. However, as nutrition education evolved, surgeons realized not all community-provided delicacies were good for all patients. One surgeon wrote a letter to the *Journal* asking local cooks and bakers not to bring fat and sugar-laden pies and pastries to the hospital without his approval.

A new type of hospital kitchen evolved during the war that tailored food and drink to patients according to their ailments. The special diet kitchen, set apart from the regular hospital kitchen, was championed by activist and reformer Annie Wittenmyer, who worked for the U.S. Christian Commission. Like the Sanitary Commission, the Christian Commission was a major civilian relief agency created to coordinate supplies for Union troops. However, as its name suggests, the Christian Commission saw its primary duty as evangelizing the armies, whereas the Sanitary Commission was more secular.

Wittenmyer's work took her straight to battlefields, and she became well acquainted with such Army generals as Ulysses S. Grant, whose camps and naval forces she frequently visited, armed with food and medical supplies. The title of Wittenmyer's Civil War memoir, *Under the Guns*, accurately describes her wartime experience, during which she often dodged bullets while traveling in horse-drawn wagons and gunboats.

She wrote about her plan for changing army hospital cuisine: "No part of the army service was so defective, during the first two years of the war, as the cooking department in the United States government hospitals. Few of the men employed as cooks in these hospitals were trained or skilled; most of them had obtained their knowledge of cookery after being assigned to duty, under most unfavorable circumstances, and without the proper facilities for doing their work. One general kitchen provided the food for all—the sick, the wounded, and the dying, as well as the nurses and convalescents."[62]

"Where there were women nurses in a hospital, and they could get a little stove of their own, special dishes were prepared for the worst patients; but there was no general system of providing dainty and suitable diet for the thousands in need of delicate food in home-like preparation. The supplies coming from the generous people of the North occasioned great anxiety."[63]

Wittenmyer came up with the idea of a special-diet kitchen system "as a flash from the skies—like a divine inspiration." She lobbied for support among both commissions, army officers and surgeons, and having secured it, set about spreading the simple plan to all the military hospitals.

Surgeons prescribed special diets for patients needing them and wrote down menus on cards assigned to patients by name and bed number. Patients would choose from a list of available foods. Wardmasters collected the menus and sent them to the special-diet kitchen supervisors, who were trained to know the appropriate types and amounts for each meal. "The food thus ordered was prepared in the special-diet kitchen, which, although under separate management, was a part of the hospital, and as completely under the control of the authorities as any other part of the hospital," she wrote.[64]

Special-diet kitchen supervisors were considered dietary nurses, not cooks. They oversaw the cooks' work. Some kitchen workers were disabled or convalescing soldiers who were not yet able or ready to rejoin their regiments.

"The food thus systematically prepared under the watchful eyes of women competent to govern such a force and direct the work, was brought to the bedside of the patients in home-like preparation," she wrote.[65]

By June, Surgeon Francis Salter had left Gallipolis and was serving as Post Hospital Surgeon in Hagerstown, Maryland. By that time, just after the first ward at Gallipolis opened, 21 sick and wounded Confederate prisoners were brought to the hospital. Union forces captured them at the Battle of Lewisburg, Greenbrier County, Virginia, and brought the prisoners to Gallipolis for treatment. It did not take long after their arrival for the Rebel patients to cause a ruckus.

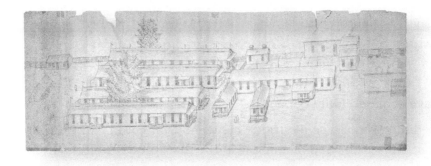

Chapter Six

REBEL PATIENTS, ROWDY VISITORS

"There are now twenty-one rebel prisoners in the hospital at Gallipolis.
Twenty-three were captured at the battle of Lewisburg; two have died since
their arrival, and one or two others are in a fair way to follow them."[66]

—*Gallipolis Journal*, July 3, 1862

Trouble was brewing in the Gallipolis general hospital wards among the Confederate prisoners of war and their visitors. Many of the patients were soldiers of the 22nd Virginia Infantry. Originally a Virginia state militia company called the Kanawha Riflemen, the 22nd was commanded by Lieutenant Colonel George Smith Patton, grandfather of World War II General George S. Patton.67

Captain William F. Bahlmann was one of the wounded 22nd Virginia officers. He recalled his stay in a military memoir, *Down in the Ranks or Bread and Blankets: An account of his military service in the Confederate Armed Forces, 1861-1865.*

> "From Charleston we were sent by boat to Gallipolis, Ohio where there was a regular military hospital. We reached Gallipolis somewhat early in the morning. I walked from the river with the officer of the guard while the others rode in an ambulance."

"As soon as I entered the hospital Mrs. Cecil, the matron, opened up on me with a full broadside. 'Here comes an officer! You are ten thousand times worse than the rest! You are the fellows that are keeping up the war!' I said, 'Madam, I don't care about this just now, but I would like to have some breakfast.' I got it."

"Our dining room was a curious sight. All that could leave their beds did so. Those that had been shot in the lower limbs would sit on a chair with the wounded limb stretched out on a stool while those that had been shot in the arm or shoulder sat close to the table. As we could not carve our meat, the matrons did it for us."

"After we had been there a few days, Pat Murray [Private Patrick Murray, 22nd Virginia] and I would be invited to a supplementary breakfast of tea and toast in the buttery. A Confederate soldier was like a young bird in a nest, his mouth always open for something to eat. When Dr. Bell, the surgeon in charge, found this out he discharged the matron. He was strict but a conscientious man."[68]

At least four of the sick and wounded Confederate soldiers transported from the Lewisburg battle died at the hospital in summer and fall of 1862. All four were buried at Gallipolis' Pine Street Cemetery. Private William F. Wickline, 50th Virginia Infantry, died as a result of a gunshot wound to the head. (His middle initial was changed to Z. on his gravestone). Three others were privates of the 22nd Virginia Infantry. Each of them was wounded in the thigh. James H. McKinney of Company G died June 19th. Robert J. Thrasher of Company I died October 1st.

The third 22nd Virginia soldier, Private Adam Samuel Rader, was admitted to the Gallipolis hospital under the wrong name. He was listed as Prisoner of War Adam S. Baden. This was no doubt a misreading of someone's penmanship. His thigh wound was not the cause of his death, as explained in this letter written to his family in Botetourt County, Virginia after his passing:

"August 10, 1862. [died] of an affection of the lungs. He was wounded and taken prisoner at Battle of Lewisburg but wound had healed. He would have fully recovered if lungs had been sound. He was well cared for in every respect and died happy. His dying message to you all was that he hoped to meet you all in heaven. He is decently buried in this place. I have seen him many times in the hospital and speak advisedly when I say that he wanted for nothing to make him comfortable. I enclose you a lock of his hair. Respectfully, Mrs. M.M. Cushing."[69]

Captain William F. Bahlmann, 22nd Virginia Infantry, C.S.A.,
Image from the book, *Down in the Ranks or Bread and Blankets: An account of his
military service in the Confederate Armed Forces, 1861-1865.*

Graves of four Confederate soldiers, wounded at the Battle of Lewisburg,
who died at Gallipolis. Photo by Steve Cunningham.

Virginians with Confederate sympathies would cross the Ohio to visit the sick and
wounded Rebel soldiers at Gallipolis. "Among them was Mr. John Steenberger,"
Bahlmann recalled, "who would talk in such a way that I cautioned him."

By August 8th, aggravated by Confederate bluster, Surgeon Bell announced that
he would no longer allow "rebels and rebel sympathizers" to visit the hospital. In
a letter to the editor of the *Journal,* he declared "All rebels and rebel sympathizers, whether male or female, will in the future be denied the privilege of visiting
the General Hospital at this place, and all communication between such persons
and prisoners of war in said Hospital, is positively forbidden."[70]

Possibly in retaliation for Bell's order, at least one patient went to the press with
complaints about his treatment at the U.S. Army General Hospital. A writer iden-
tifying himself only as "C." sent a letter to the *Cincinnati Commercial* on August
18, 1862, which was published under the headline "Tell Us the Reason Why."

> "Editors Com.—Will you, or someone who knows, tell us the reason
> why it is that, despite all orders, men who are unfit for duty must
> be detained in hospitals one weary month after another, until all the
> patience they ever had is entirely worn out? There are now in this
> hospital fifty or more of us who have been in hospitals from three to
> ten months, and have been for months pronounced hopelessly unfit
> for service; and of lives, that of hospital imprisonment, is the most

unendurable. Suspended between camp, with its duties and sports, on the one hand, and home, with its associations and pleasures, on the other, we are halted between two places—no life, no joke, nothing new, nothing pleasant: one unending, dreary, loathsome, unbearable monotony, subject to the oppressions and insults of all the petty, brainless lick-spittles who crowd themselves into positions, from ward-master to water-closet waiters."

Additional grave marker for Private Adam Samuel Rader.
Photo by Steve Cunningham.

"C." continued his diatribe by alleging that the hospital steward might have been stealing food meant for patients:

> "This country is full of fruits and all kinds of vegetables that are pleasant to the eye and good to the taste, and yet we always find the same unchanging fare at the table. It is true that now and then some good soul does bring something new and good, but the rules forbid that they should be brought farther than the office of the Steward; and from that office to our table there is no means of transportation."[71]

Harper caught wind of the Cincinnati letter and posited in *The Journal* that complaints against Dr. Bell's leadership were leveled by "a certain class, whose secession proclivities have compelled the Surgeon in Charge to place a check upon their promulgation in the hospital itself."[72]

Dr. Bell took a shot of his own at "C." in a letter to the *Commercial:*

> "Editors Com:-A moment's notice of C.'s communication, under the caption of 'Tell Us the Reason Why,' dated U.S. Military Hospital, Gallipolis, Ohio, Aug. 18, 1862. The public might suppose that I am responsible for the non-discharge of those fifty men who have been so cruelly imprisoned in hospitals for so long a time; but I am not. Those men were sent here from Wheeling on the 15th day of July, with orders for me to discharge such as should be discharged, and send such as were fit for service to their regiments. I made up all their papers within the first ten days and they are now at General Headquarters to be endorsed."

> "If ward-masters and others have been insolent (which I do not believe), C. should have complained to me, not to you. If C. is starving, let him come to me and I will have his wants supplied."

> "C. falsifies if he says that delicacies for the sick and wounded were appropriated by the Steward and others. I am the judge of what men should eat, not outsiders or the sick themselves. Our table is supplied with fresh bread, fresh beef, butter, eggs, apples, potatoes, tomatoes, green corn, rice, chickens, milk, molasses, sugar, tea, coffee, berries etc., etc., in fact all the market affords."

> "Will C. give me his name? He will if he has no axe to grind. I challenge a full investigation. Come one, come all, and see for yourself, and in the future let C., whether he be a patient or a toper, or some poor rebel sympathizer, come to me with his complaints and I will arrange it to the satisfaction of all concerned."

> — James R. Bell, Acting Assistant Surgeon, U.S.A. in charge.[73]

We cannot be sure from available information whether Dr. Bell faced direct repercussions after "C.'s" complaint was published, but in October, Dr. O.E. Davis of the 119th Ohio Volunteer Infantry replaced Bell as Surgeon in Charge. Bell remained at the hospital as Acting Assistant Surgeon and also lent a hand in the hospital's business office.

Two new assistant surgeons arrived that fall. Dr. Fred Cromley reported for duty after serving as a field hospital assistant surgeon and druggist. He had enlisted in the army while still a medical student at the Cincinnati College of Medicine and Surgery.

In November, Bell's Ohio 7th comrade, Charles C. Bosworth, was transferred from the Charleston Post Hospital to Gallipolis, once again uniting Bell, whose life was in danger at Charleston, and the nurse who cared for him.

Private Charles C. Bosworth, 7th Ohio Volunteer Infantry,
Hospital Steward, Druggist & Wardmaster.
Image courtesy Gallia County Historical Society

Chapter Seven

A DRUMMER BOY, DROUGHT, AND A DELUGE OF REFUGEES

"From an eyewitness, we have received a reliable account of the battle at Fayette...A late instance has come to our knowledge, which occurred after the fight between Col. Loring's rebels and the 34th and 47th O.V. [Ohio Volunteers] at Fayette Court House in Western Virginia, under Cols. Seibur and Toland. The wounded were placed in ambulances for transportation to Gauley. The miscreants attacked the ambulances, shot the horses, drivers, and wounded soldiers. A little drummer boy, walking behind one of the ambulances, was shot by these wretches, and is now at the hospital in this place."[74]

—*Gallipolis Journal*, September 18, 1862

Eleven-year-old Joseph Russell Wheeler was not actually wounded in the attack, but bushwhackers shot his drum right out of his hands. He suffered a powder burn on his nose from the bullet that barely missed him. He was a musician with the 9th Virginia Infantry (US). He and his father, Company H Captain Joseph C. Wheeler, enlisted on the same October day in 1861 at Ceredo, Virginia. His extreme youth and small size—he measured only four feet, seven inches—did not keep him from joining the regiment, though one can assume his father permitted him to enlist.[75]

Although he was not wounded in Fayette County, drummer boy Wheeler ended up sick, as reported, at the U.S. Army General Hospital at Gallipolis in the fall of 1862. Dr. Bell examined him in August 1862 and wrote this of his condition:

> "I certify that I have carefully examined the said Joseph Russel [sic] Wheeler, a musician of Captain J.C. Wheeler's Company and find him incapable of performing the duties of a soldier... Debilitated. Digestion very much impaired. Erysipelas (severe bacterial infection) in both legs. Anasarca (tissue swelling due to fluid retention) of both legs and feet. Is very slight in person, not as robust as the average of boys at the same age, and physically not able to do military duty."[76]

Pvt. Joseph R. Wheeler, 9th Virginia (West Virginia) Infantry,
image from ancestry.com

Dr. Bell discharged Joseph on a certificate of disability at the ripe old age of 12. According to newspaper reports, the little drummer boy whose instrument was blasted by Rebel fire "reported the loss of his drum and the governor took him to an army supply base to get another. He picked out the one he liked best and the governor wrote his name on it."[77] As it was 1862, before western Virginia became the state of West Virginia, that governor would have been Francis Harrison Pierpont, the governor of the Restored Government of Virginia. The first governor of the new state was Arthur I. Boreman, elected in 1863.[78]

Wheeler went on to attend Marshall College at Huntington, West Virginia, marry and raise a large family. He was 74 when he died, and his obituary stated that he was the youngest veteran of the Civil War.

Although Dr. Bell's work at that point consisted almost entirely of signing and issuing paperwork, including casualty lists and certificates of discharge due to disability, he also reported several Gallipolis patient cases to the U.S. Surgeon General's office. Surgeon General Joseph K. Barnes issued an 1862 order stipulating that army medical directors provide "all obtainable statistics and data in connection with past and future operations of those armies, which may be essential or useful in the accurate compilation of the Medical and Surgical History of the War." The information became a series of volumes titled *The Medical and Surgical History of the War of the Rebellion.*

Dr. Bell contributed to Volume Two in the chapter "Gunshot Contusions of the Cranial Bones." He reported that Private William Wallace, 23rd Ohio Volunteers, sustained a gunshot scalp wound at the Battle of Antietam, Maryland. He was treated and returned to duty with his regiment but was soon taken from the field and admitted to the General Hospital at Gallipolis after developing epileptic convulsions. Wallace's case added important data to then-evolving medical knowledge about depressed skull fractures, which often led to soldiers suffering epileptic seizures.[79]

Later that fall, Confederate Private Robert Thrasher, who had been brought to Gallipolis with a gunshot wound in the thigh after the Lewisburg battle, died at the hospital. According to his obituary, Thrasher left behind a wife and three children, none of whom were old enough when he died to remember him. He is buried at the Pine Street Cemetery in Gallipolis, where Confederate graves were not initially decorated along with those of Union soldiers.[80] Hannah Maxon would later have a hand in changing that practice.

> "Gallipolis is surely the city of Good Samaritans, for the inhabitants not only brought all the delicacies of the season to our brave, patriotic sick

and wounded soldiers from the Kanawha, but generously threw open their residences. To all such I desire to express my heartfelt thanks, and more particularly so to Mr. Drouillard, Sr., and daughter; Mr. and Mrs. Harper of the *Gallipolis Journal;* Dr. Early; Mrs. Wilson, the landlady of the Valley House, and Dr. O.E. Davis of Lancaster, Ohio, for their unremitting attentions and acts of kindness to my poor, wounded boy, Johnny Packham, Thirty-fourth Regiment, Ohio (First Zouaves)."

—Mrs. Esther Packham, Sept. 30, 1862[81]

Private Robert J. Thrasher, 22nd Virginia Infantry CSA
Image courtesy of Howard R. Hammond

With Doctor Gabriel departing in the fall of 1862, the team of Surgeons Oliver E. Davis and James R. Bell were at the hospital's helm and Charles Bosworth served as hospital steward. Unlike the excessive rains of the previous fall, though, a drought was parching the Ohio Valley that impacted the supply of available fruits and vegetables. "Corn in many places is about dried up," read one report. "Pasture is in many places literally burnt out. Fruit is suffering also from the heat of the sun."

The rhythm and flow of daily life in Civil War Gallipolis quickened, with people flooding into town. An increasing number of escaped slaves, known in military terms as contrabands, were crossing over into Ohio and traveling on to locations further into the state to find farm work. Their journey toward the state's interior was said to make them feel safer than they might be staying in Gallipolis, so close to the Virginia border.[82]

In late November, Hannah became President of the Ladies' Soldiers' Aid Society in addition to her nursing duties. Her mother Eliza hosted the group's meeting that month at their home. Their primary mission was to provide Ohio Union soldiers with blankets and clothing, but they also accepted cash donations for supplies.[83]

By Christmas, there were 230 soldiers in the hospital. Surgeon Davis arranged a Christmas dinner, aided by local cooks. "Although the notice was short, yet many nobly responded to the call of Dr. Davis, and ably seconded his efforts to make the sick and convalescent soldiers under his charge as happy as possible. The result was that 214 surrounded a table loaded with every delicacy of the season, particularly turkey and oysters, to all of which they did ample justice."[84]

It was a moment of much needed holiday peace. But no one around that hospital dining hall table could have predicted that Rebel forces would make it to Ohio soil in the new year.

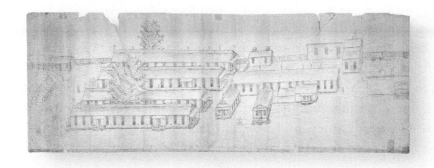

Chapter Eight

A MILITARY MURDER

"I now know what war is."

—William Waddell Mills, Assistant Surgeon, 18th OVI

In early January 1863, Surgeon and Gallipolis native William W. Mills wrote to the *Journal* about his regiment's fight in the Battle of Stones River, near Murfreesboro, Tennessee.

> "The battle took place on the north side of Stone's river, three miles from Murfreesboro, and commenced on Tuesday morning [December 31st, 1862], and lasted until Saturday night, with intervals of quiet. The hard fighting was done on Wednesday, Thursday, and Friday. Our division, brigade, and regiment was engaged in the hottest of it during those three days. Col. [Timothy R.] Stanley commanding our brigade did nobly. Twice did our division save our army. They stood firm while others ran away."

> "Many of our boys have had limbs amputated. I have stood by the operating table and amputated limbs when my feet were in blood an inch deep. I have had a hundred eyes turned upon me at once, and as many voices, each asking to have his wounds dressed first. Oh the horrors of a hospital on a battlefield, are past description."

"There was but little fighting on Saturday, and none yesterday [Sunday]. No fighting this morning. Our advance is moving into Murfreesboro without opposition. The enemy is gone, and we are not able to pursue. We have lost in prisoners perhaps two or three thousand, and have taken of the enemy about as many. I came near being captured several times, and several times found myself mixed up with flying bullets and bursting shells. I now know what war is."

Yours, W.W. Mills, Assistant Surgeon,
18th Reg., O.V.I.[85]

Assistant Surgeon William W. Mills,
18th Ohio Volunteer Infantry.
Image courtesy Bossard Memorial Library, Gallipolis, Ohio

On the February day Hospital Steward Joseph Lunbeck arrived for duty in Gallipolis, hogs were running free in the city, kicking up slush and muck created by warming winter temperatures, gouging muddy roads with their snouts and hooves. Lunbeck walked into the hospital office to learn that there were over 300 patients in the wards and a severe hospital water shortage.

Although there was a well on hospital grounds, there was no good way for workers to draw enough up for the hospital's increasing daily needs. An opinion piece in the *Journal* laid out the inefficient method being used to bring supplemental river water to the hospital. "Two water carts with two horses in each, and two men are daily employed hauling water from the wharf, 1 ¼ miles to supply the wants of 300 men... Two cisterns were made at the hospital, but so badly done as to be of no service...An ample supply of pure water is indispensable to the health of the sick soldiers. River water is frequently muddy and in summer, and to persons unaccustomed to its use, very unpleasant."[86] Harper asserted that the Army Quartermaster at Gallipolis could surely come up with a better system.

In the war's midst, another type of bloodshed stained both the town and its military hospital. Private James Driver of the 4th West Virginia Infantry had been a patient at the Army hospital. After recuperating from illness, he enlisted in the Invalid Corps (its name was later changed to the Veteran Reserve Corps) which was a Union military branch that allowed partially disabled or otherwise unfit soldiers to work light duty jobs at the general hospitals.

Driver was able enough to go to town and got permission to do so. According to news reports, the private began drinking after his arrival. He was visibly intoxicated when he stopped into Hanks' Grocery on Pine Street and asked to buy some liquor. The grocer refused to sell him any, Driver then insulted Hanks' wife and Hanks ordered him to leave the store. Driver refused to get out, so Hanks called a policeman. The soldier then hit Police Officer George Weaver and Weaver hit Driver back, smashing him with a pound weight.

Enraged, the bloodied, drunken soldier vowed to return and shoot the officer. Driver went to the hospital, somehow got his hands on his gun (which should have been kept from him in storage) and returned to the store. He shot Weaver, who was sitting on the doorstep of the grocery store, and the officer died within a half-hour.[87]

"Thus has another of our citizens been murdered in open day, and a good soldier, through the influence of whiskey, placed himself in a situation where his own life is in imminent peril," wrote Harper. "We envy not the feelings of the grog-seller, who, for a paltry half dime, furnished the fiery poison, under the influence of which this crime was committed."[88]

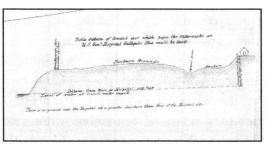

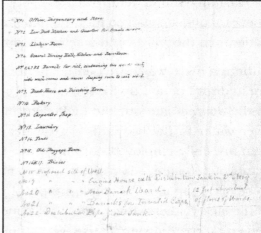

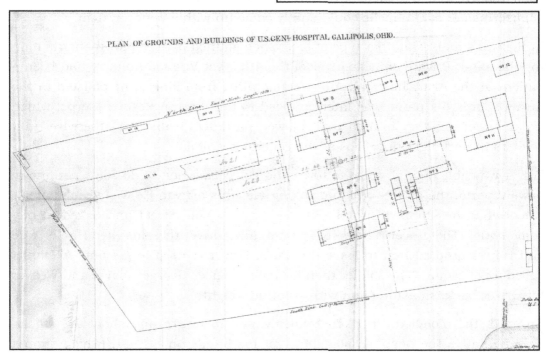

Plan of grounds and buildings of U.S. General Hospital, Gallipolis, Ohio.
National Archives

Police arrested Driver and threw him in jail. That fall, he was found guilty of manslaughter, convicted in Gallia County Common Pleas Court, and sentenced to one year in the Ohio Penitentiary. A legal notice appeared in the December issues of the *Journal,* announcing that an application for Driver's pardon would be sent to the Governor of Ohio in early 1864. Jane Driver, presumably a wife or other relative, signed the notice. James Driver later applied for an Army pension, which was denied in November 1889, on the grounds that he was dishonorably discharged from the service, September 21, 1863, "by reason of his conviction of crime by the civil authority."[89]

Citizen complaints about soldier patients made their way into the pages of the *Journal* around that time. Harper referred to "hospital rats" who were up to no good, debauchery, drinking, violence, and the like. "Many of them seem to have entered the service only for plunder, or to be supported at hospitals."[90]

Dr. Bell, who once again became Surgeon in Charge that spring, rebutted the paper's claims that all drunken soldiers carousing in town were from the hospital. "There has not been at any time, within the period above named, more than eight or ten men in hospital who would get drunk," he wrote in a letter to the *Journal.*[91]

There had been hope that spring, among members of the Gallia County War Committee, that the war would soon be over. They watched "the recent reversals of the rebel arms in West Virginia, as the forerunner of the speedy downfall of the rebellion."[92] But that summer, Rebel troops led by Confederate General John Hunt Morgan breached Ohio's border. Morgan and his raiders entered Gallia County at Vinton and rode on to Centerville. As Morgan approached, Gallipolis militiamen flocked to the city to protect the "vast amount of quartermaster and commissary goods" stored there.

Local militia units and Union soldiers pursued Morgan, forcing him to retreat to Buffington Island in the Ohio River between Meigs County, Ohio, and Jackson County, West Virginia. From there, Morgan escaped to Columbiana County, Ohio, where he was captured by Union forces. He was taken to the Ohio Penitentiary at Columbus, escaped that prison by tunneling out, and was subsequently killed in Tennessee. The Battle of Buffington Island was the only significant Civil War battle fought in Ohio. Morgan's infiltration of the state became commonly known as Morgan's Raid.[93]

Also that summer, Ohio Governor David Tod received authorization to raise one regiment of colored troops in Ohio. Newspaperman Harper wrote an editorial encouraging the African American free men of Gallia County to sign up.[94] Meanwhile, Massachusetts Surgeon Lincoln R. Stone was Assistant Surgeon of the 54th Massachusetts Infantry, one of the first two United States Colored Troops regiments assembled in the country. Famed orator and abolitionist Frederick Douglass helped recruit soldiers for the 54th and 55th Massachusetts U.S.C.T.[95]

In April 1863, Stone was on duty with the 54th at the Siege of Fort Wagner, Morris Island, Charleston, South Carolina. After the fighting ended, Dr. Stone was in communication with "Boston editors," and was quoted as saying, "I really think they showed themselves very brave, true soldiers in both of the engagements they have been in." Two serious fights within two days "have gone far to remove whatever prejudice may have existed in this department against colored troops."[96]

On June 20th, 1863, the United States officially admitted fifty western Virginia counties to the Union, and five more counties joined after that date to create the new, thirty-fifth state, West Virginia. Ohio finally had a Union-loyal neighbor across the river. Also that summer, Steward Lunbeck married his sweetheart, Agnes Truslow of Charleston, West Virginia, at Gallipolis.[97]

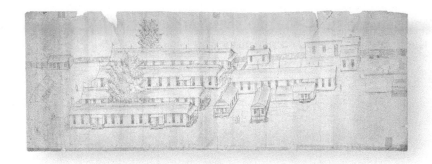

Chapter Nine

HOLY HEALERS

*"In about half an hour or so, the nurses came to take him into the operating room.
As he was carried out, he said: 'Farewell, boys! farewell!'. In two hours afterward he
breathed his last! As I watched by him for a few minutes—a few minutes, reader,
for I went from one dying man to another, and from the bedside of the dying to
the grave, and from the grave to the bedside again—O God! this is war!"*

—Reverend W.W. Lyle, Chaplain,
11th Regiment O.V.I., in his memoir *Lights and Shadows of Army Life*[98]

I n addition to caring for soldiers' physical health, Army hospital chaplains
worked to provide patients with spiritual and educational well-being. In
1863, Chaplain Charles M. Blake was stationed at the Gallipolis hospital. He
reported to the American Tract Society at Boston that he had passed around an
assortment of religious pamphlets and papers that the Society had provided him,
"so that there should be something different for each ward and the patients could
exchange, till all had read what each had received." He also made an appeal to
readers of his report to send books to the hospital, for the patients he described
as "famishing for them."[99]

An 1862 Act of Congress authorized the President of the United States to appoint
a Chaplain for each Permanent Hospital, "whose pay, with that of chaplains of
hospitals heretofore appointed by him, shall be the same as that of regimental chaplains in the volunteer force."[100] Two years later, Congress voted to raise

hospital chaplain pay to 100 dollars per month and two daily rations, which put them on the same footing as some army officers.

Rev. Charles M. Blake, Chaplain, U.S. Army Hospital,
Gallipolis, OH, 1862-1863.
Image courtesy CivilWarTalk blog

The editor of the *Urbana* (Ohio) *Union* did not agree with this pay increase for chaplains. In a February 1864 opinion piece, he wrote: "To the faithful and devoted chaplain who follows his men and shares with them their toils and dangers, tends the sick and wounded, and is in every way the soldier's friend and adviser, too much honor cannot be awarded, and his influence for good with the soldiers can hardly be overestimated. But such men go into their work for a higher than earthly reward, and cannot be bought with money; and the proposed increase of salary will be as injurious in its effects on the service, as it is unwise in an economical point of view, in the present condition of our expenses."[101]

Despite such views, Congress approved the pay raise. There is no question that chaplains, along with other hospital and regimental staff, were exposed to great dangers on and off the battlefields and in the hospitals. Rev. Russell G. French, who was chaplain of the 23rd Ohio Volunteer Infantry, ended up as a patient at Gallipolis after being shot in a western Virginia skirmish. He was transported down the Kanawha and Ohio on the steamer Mary Cook, suffering from a gunshot wound. Editor Harper wrote: "He is doing well, and with the kind treatment he will receive at the hands of our able hospital surgeon, and the ministering angels, the ladies, will soon be on his pegs again."[102]

23rd O.V.I. Lieutenant Colonel Rutherford B. Hayes delivered a much more worrisome assessment of French's condition, writing that he was possibly mortally wounded and "crippled for life." Hayes wrote to Ohio Governor David Tod, requesting that he officially commission French as Regimental Chaplain since he had been shot while on a company scout.

> "Mr. French is a loyal citizen of Mercer County [Virginia], of unblemished character, and with a fair reputation as a Christian and clergyman. He was driven from his home because he was a Union man; joined my command at Raleigh to act as guide and scout. We found him a most valuable man. He served without compensation... He has a large family and small means. Officers and men all desire his appointment as herein requested."

Governor Tod did commission Rev. French. Hayes continued to monitor the chaplain's condition and expressed concern for his welfare in several diary entries and letters to his wife. Just after he was promoted to Colonel, Hayes visited French and other soldiers at Gallipolis. "Had a nice trip up the river," he wrote to his wife Lucy. "Mr. French and eight men in hospital, all glad to see me."[103] Russell G. French was discharged for disability the following year. He received an Army pension until his death in December 1905.

In his monthly report on his duties at the U.S. Army General Hospital at Parkersburg, West Virginia, Chaplain L. H. Monroe wrote: "I have continued my usual daily visits to the wards, have continued to preach twice on the Sabbath, and kept up my regular Prayer Meetings and Bible Class during the week."[104] Chaplain James H. Brown of the U.S.A. General Hospital in Beaufort, South Carolina, likewise affirmed that he had "good reason to believe that under the influence of Divine Services and social meetings a number [of patients] have greatly improved their Spiritual conditions."[105]

Steering soldiers along the spiritual straight and narrow was a journey often strewn with temptation. Rev. Blake was up against such obstacles in early 1864, when reports surfaced of "Scores of abandoned women" who were seen around the hills and riverbank, "making night hideous with their debauchery and drunkenness, and even in daylight it is hardly safe for respectable persons to pass along the river road."[106] An opinion in the *Journal* called for "... more stringent means to be adopted to drive off these miserable creatures who hang around the hospitals in order to associate with those soldiers who are degraded enough to seek their company."[107]

Rutherford B. Hayes, commander of the 23rd Ohio Infantry and
future nineteenth president of the United States
Library of Congress

Evidence of soldiers consorting with "abandoned women," a nineteenth century euphemism for prostitutes, showed up at around that time on the muster roll card of a patient, a private of the Ninth Virginia Infantry: "In hospital, Gallipolis, Ohio. [Pay] Stop for loss of time on account of having the Gonorrhea, $6.50."[108]

"Dear Mr. Shaw:

I cannot tell you the sadness I feel at having to write you that your son is missing—certainly, a prisoner, wounded—perhaps dead in the hands of the enemy. He fell Saturday night, in the unsuccessful assault upon Fort Wagner, while leading the regiment, having reached the top of the parapet. He was last seen waving his sword to the men, calling on them to follow him, and either fell or leaped into the Fort and was not seen again."

—Dr. Lincoln R. Stone, Surgeon, 54th Massachusetts United States Colored Troops, in a letter to the father of Colonel Robert G. Shaw from Morris Island, SC, July 21, 1863[109]

Surgeon Lincoln R. Stone, 2nd & 54th Massachusetts Infantry, Surgeon-in-charge USAGH, Gallipolis, Ohio. Image courtesy John Appleton Collection, West Virginia & Regional History Center, West Virginia University

In mid-January 1864, the War Department issued General Orders Number 23, overturning the Army's previous rules regarding employment of black men and women in hospitals. "The employment of persons of African descent, male or female, as cooks or nurses, will be permitted in all U.S. General Hospitals. When so employed they will receive ten dollars per month and one ration. They will be paid by the nearest Medical Disbursing Officer, on rolls similar to those used in the payment of men of the Hospital Corps."[110]

Soon after the government issued the new order, Reuben West, an African American, was hired as a cook at the U.S. Army Hospital in Gallipolis. Three months later, he was paid for additional work as a contract nurse.[111] West's work included feeding and caring for 184 patients.

By January 31st, 1864, just months after the death of his comrade and friend Colonel Robert Gould Shaw in South Carolina, Surgeon Lincoln R. Stone wrote to Brig. Gen. Lorenzo Thomas that he was on duty at the U.S. Army General Hospital at Gallipolis. He relieved Acting Assistant Surgeon James Bell.[112] On February 14, 1864, 31-year-old Lincoln, married Harriet Hodges, 28, of Salem, Massachusetts. The surgeon's father, Rev. Thomas T. Stone, performed the ceremony in Salem.[113]

Right after the wedding, Dr. and Mrs. Stone left New England for Ohio and took up residence on the Gallipolis hospital grounds. A Pennsylvania soldier wrote about the hospital and its new surgeon in charge: "The hospital is located on high ground, the buildings enclosed by a high fence, and kept in order with scrupulous care. It contains some seven hundred patients, among them are many of the Invalid Corps. The grounds are about six acres in extent, the buildings substantial frames. In one of them resides the resident surgeon, Dr. Lincoln Stone, a physician highly spoken of by the men."[114]

An article in the *Gallipolis Journal* noted Dr. Stone's leadership. "The hospital grounds now contain 20 acres, about 15 of which are cultivated as a garden and from present appearance will furnish a large supply of vegetables. Dr. L.R. Stone, Surg. U.S. Vols, is now in charge. Drs. Bell, Banta, Levisay [this is a misspelling of the name Livesay], Mills, Rathbone [misspelling of Rathburn] and Phillips are daily in attendance in the various wards."[115]

The Dr. Mills named in the article was Surgeon William Waddell Mills, who, after being discharged for disability from his regiment three years into the war, joined the staff at Gallipolis as a contract surgeon at about the same time Joseph Lunbeck came on.

Lunbeck submitted a Steward's report for the month of March 1864 to Col. Joseph K. Barnes, Acting Surgeon General, U.S.A. He was listed as Hospital Steward, along with Charles C. Bosworth, in April 1864. That month, the hospital employed five female nurses and eight cooks. There were 189 vacant beds out of a total 500 available. Eighty-six patients were admitted, six were returned to duty, one was transferred, one was furloughed, no patients discharged, one patient deserted, two died and 311 patients remained.[116]

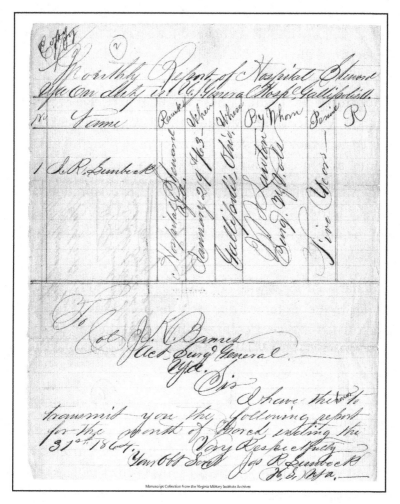

Hospital Steward's Report of Joseph Lunbeck, March 1864.
Manuscript Collection, Virginia Military Institute Archives

On the morning of May 9th, 1864, Union and Confederate forces under the commands of Generals George Crook and Albert Gallatin Jenkins respectively, clashed at Cloyd's Mountain in southwestern Virginia. "The contest was short, sharp and decisive," a correspondent for the *Wheeling Daily Intelligencer* wrote. "Volley after volley of musketry was poured in, at short range and with deadly precision." According to this reporter, 500 Union troops were killed and wounded, while the Confederate forces lost 900 killed, wounded, and taken prisoner.[117]

The following day there was another battle at New River Bridge. Chief Medical Director for the Union, Surgeon George M. Kellogg, reported on the Cloyd's Mountain and New River Bridge wounded:

> "...in assaulting their strong position at Cloyd's Mountain, our force suffered severely. Having been engaged for several hours in collecting our wounded from the field and in attending to their wounds, I was ordered to follow the command with all the wounded I could transport."

> "We had but thirty-eight ambulances in all, only twelve of which were in good condition. We arrived at Meadow Bluff [West Virginia] on the 21st. I was ordered to remove the wounded at once to hospital at Charleston, West Virginia, and to Gallipolis, Ohio, which I accordingly did."

> "I took one hundred and ninety-two wounded to hospital at Gallipolis, Ohio, and to Charleston, [West] Virginia, all of which were cases of wounds of the arm, forearm, hand and feet or flesh wounds of more or less grave character."[118]

30-year-old Zachariah Nicely was one of those wounded. He was captured at Cloyd's Mountain by Rebel forces and held for ten days. The Fayetteville, West Virginia farmer-turned-sergeant escaped and joined the caravan headed for hospitals. He made it to Gallipolis, one of 120 soldiers treated there, where he underwent surgery. His left arm was amputated.[119]

The influx of patients and increasing numbers of visitors forced Dr. Stone to issue a request to all concerned:

> "*Editor Journal:* Will you oblige me by informing the citizens of Gallipolis and vicinity, that for the present, visitors will only be allowed to enter the Hospital between the hours of three and five o'clock P.M. Sunday, Monday, Wednesday, and Friday. This arrangement is necessary from the large number of sick and wounded, many of them severe cases. Visitors would also confer a great favor by not bringing articles of food with them, such as pies, pastry &c. Nothing of this sort should be given to patients without the permission of the attending surgeons."

> L. R. Stone, Surgeon U.S.V. In charge Hos.[120]

Patient numbers surged again following the June Battle of Lynchburg, a Confederate victory that forced Union Generals David Hunter and George Crook into a massive retreat across West Virginia. Most of the injured of the 91st Ohio Volunteer Infantry, a southwestern Ohio regiment, were taken to Gallipolis under harrowing circumstances.

A member of the regiment wrote: "The wounded although transported over a rough road nearly 200 miles are generally doing well, and have had every attention paid them which it was possible to give, on a forced march, night and day, in order to reach supplies of which the army was entirely out, and none to be had by foraging in a country already twice passed over by our army."[121]

A 91st Ohio Volunteer Infantry corporal added these details: "The night before the battle of Lynchburg there was issued to each man a cracker and a half. This was the evening of the 18th and we got no more until Monday night June 27th, in the meantime we lived on beef and nothing else. I did not dream I should ever live to see men eat grass like animals, but on the night of the 25th, I saw men in my company go into a field and cut clover and eat like a horse."[122]

One soldier's separation from his unit after Lynchburg caused him financial distress. Writing from the U.S. General Hospital at Gallipolis to the Adjutant General, he explained that he was wounded in the battle. "I have written to the commander of my company several times. I presume that the company books is lost. I have not got any pay for 11 months. My family is in suffering condition. The head segt. here in the hospital written to my Regt., he says that he cannot git it. I hope this will meet your approbation, Edward Hanrahan, Company C, 34 Regt. O. Vol."[123]

In the early days of Dr. Stone's tenure at U.S. Army General Hospital at Gallipolis, he issued an updated set of rules regarding chain of command in the aftermath of hospital deaths. This is an excerpt from that correspondence, found at the National Library of Medicine Historical Medical Collection, Bethesda, Maryland: "When a patient dies, the Head Nurse will furnish the attending Surgeon with a list of all the effects of the deceased to be embraced in the 'report of death.' Money and valuables will be given to the Surgeon in Charge, for safe keeping and the other articles handed over to the Steward in Charge of Kept Property." Hannah and the other nurses were responsible, in such cases, for removing the deceased's bedding and clothing and taking them to the soiled clothes room.[124]

Corporal Joseph Lunbeck applied for discharge due to disability to Dr. Stone, who forwarded the request to Northern Department Medical Director Charles S.

Tripler. Tripler granted the discharge but had no replacement steward to send to Gallipolis at the time. "Having no steward in the Department who can be spared from present duties I have made application to Col. Wood, Ass't Surgeon General for a detail of an intelligent steward to report to you."[125]

Lunbeck was discharged for disability at Gallipolis on June 22, 1864. By July 20th, Max Joseph Koenig was transferred from the U.S. General Hospital at Covington, Kentucky, to Gallipolis to replace Lunbeck. Koenig had some formal medical education. "I have attended one course of regular lectures, and also kept the situation as Hospital Steward in the 1st Regiment New Jersey Militia," he wrote in an application letter for a previous job in a Washington, D.C., Army hospital.[126]

In a letter of recommendation for Koenig, a regimental chaplain wrote of him, "The bearer, M. Jos. Koenig, was our Hospital Steward (1st Regt, N.J. Inf) during his three months' service. He gave great satisfaction and was quite popular. I can recommend him highly in all regards, and especially as being eminently qualified for the post of Hospital Steward."[127]

Seven patients died at the hospital during the week of June 30th through July 3rd alone, and that toll rose to eleven deaths two weeks later, at a time when there were nearly 800 patients in the wards. One, a Pennsylvania soldier who was said to be "laboring under temporary insanity," escaped from the hospital, headed to the river and drowned.[128] In an attempt to lift the spirits of the living, Hannah and other local ladies organized a hospital Fourth of July dinner.[129]

The town was not in its usual celebratory mood that Independence Day. The *Journal* reported, "The 4th of July passed off in Gallipolis, very quietly, and without anything to indicate it as a day formerly honored and universally celebrated. The 172nd Reg. Ohio National Guard paraded in the morning, and made quite a fine appearance. Some fine flags were hung out, and a few rounds of cannon fired, but taken as a whole, the day was as quiet as any other. Our people have daily evidence of the stern realities of this war. Particularly is this the case just now. With a hospital crowded full of sick and wounded soldiers and the roll of the muffled drum daily sounding in their ears, as some brave here is taken to his final resting place, they do not feel that the time of rejoicing has yet arrived."[130]

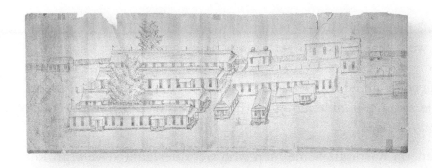

Chapter Ten

ABSENT WITHOUT LEAVE

*"The attention of Deserters from the Ninth Regiment Virginia Volunteer
Infantry directed to a list published in another column. Boys, you had better
comply with Major Darr's request, and report yourselves forthwith
for duty. The Major is terribly in earnest."*[131]

—*Gallipolis Journal,* January 1, 1863

By early 1863, increasing numbers of soldiers from both sides were deserting their units. It was common for troops to straggle behind their regiments after battles, and not all of those absences were true desertions. But many were, and among those who were wounded or became sick, hospital transport sometimes enabled their escapes.

The United States War Department issued orders for policing those separated from their regiments. General Order Number 72 stated that "Whenever sick men, paroled prisoners or others, under circumstances entitling them to their descriptive lists and accounts of pay and clothing, etc., are sent away from their regiments, or, point to point in a body, they will be put in charge of a trusty officer or non-commissioned officer—to be selected, if possible, from their own number—who will exercise command over the party and conduct it to its destination."[132]

Those rules worked only under ideal conditions. In *Desertion During the Civil War,* Ella Lonn wrote about hospital desertions: "Furloughs and sick leaves at a hospital inevitably offered temptation, especially if, as frequently happened, patients were discharged to return to their commands without a guard. As in every army, some feigned illness or wounds, and were thus enabled to wander off. It was complained by [General Robert E.] Lee that they filled the houses of the charitable and hospitable along the line of march. Discharge from the hospitals was greatly abused."[133]

At the general hospitals some men who were designated Veteran Reserve Corps members—those wounded or disabled unfit for duty—served as guards. Even so, a few patients escaped the hospital grounds.

One of the slipperiest soldiers was Martin Sowards. A Lawrence County, Ohio native, Sowards was 18 years old when he enlisted in the Ninth Virginia Infantry [US]. At the time he was admitted to the Gallipolis Army hospital, he was enlisted in the Third West Virginia Cavalry, although records show he was probably a private in the First Ohio Heavy Artillery of the 117th Ohio Infantry. He is listed in the Weekly Report of U.S. General Hospital, Gallipolis, Ohio, for the week ending January 23, 1864 as part of that regiment. A week later, he was listed as a deserter from the hospital.[134]

His story is remarkable for the number of times he enlisted in different Virginia, West Virginia, and Ohio regiments, and for the number of times he deserted from hospitals and escaped from prison. A notation on a Descriptive List of Deserters Arrested, dated February 1864, reads: "$30 reward for arrest. This man has been in three different regiments in 9th Virginia Infantry, 3rd Virginia Cavalry and 117th Ohio Volunteer Infantry." On top of all of those enlistments, desertions, and arrests, he was sentenced to Atheneum Prison at Wheeling, West Virginia, to serve hard labor; he escaped from that jail as well.[135]

Under certain circumstances, surgeons in charge were ordered to confine hospital deserters who were court-martialed. In the case of Private J.C. Rupe of the 2nd West Virginia Cavalry, who had been court-martialed and found guilty of absence without leave, the sentence was "fatigue duty" at the hospital for ten days.[136]

In an 1864 case, 2nd West Virginia Cavalry Private Joseph Metcalf was arrested and tried at Camp Brough barracks near Gallipolis. He was brought before a garrison court martial on charges of absence without leave, drunkenness, and "having in his possession articles of citizens' clothing to enable him to escape the guard lines of the U.S. General Hospital, Gallipolis, Ohio." He was found guilty and sentenced "to be confined and fed on bread and water only, for eight consecutive days at U.S. General Hospital... The prisoner will be relieved from confinement and sent under guard to U.S. General Hospital, Gallipolis, Ohio, and there delivered to Surgeon L.R. Stone, U.S. Vols in Charge, who will see that the sentence is duly executed."[137]

In June 1864, a contingent of Ohio State inspectors visited the hospital, tasked with reporting back to Governor Brough on the conditions of the patients there. At the time of the agents' visit, the hospital grounds had grown to 29 acres, about half of which was a vegetable garden whose harvest was used to feed the patients.

According to their report, there were then 562 patients, 216 of whom were Ohioans representing nineteen different regiments.

> "All of them seemed to be as comfortable as possible to make men under like circumstances. There are no cases of a serious character, and in a short time, many will be sufficiently restored to return to duty."

> "Friends of Ohio soldiers in this hospital may rest assured that every possible care is taken of them; far beyond what they could receive if at home. Sanitary stores are bountifully supplied. An inexhaustible supply of ice was secured last winter and in short everything which kindness can prompt or money procure is furnished without stint."

> "There are in the hospital from West Virginia regiments, 300 men and boys, 126 of whom are from the 13th Regiment Virginia Infantry. Of this latter number, we found about 45 boys varying from 13 to 17 years of age, utterly broken down in constitution and rendered unserviceable for life. Dr. Stone, surgeon in charge, has forwarded applications for their immediate discharge."[138]

At least one of those soldiers stayed on at Gallipolis as a hospital cook. 33-year-old Ezekiel Wilson, a dark-haired farmer from Meigs County, Ohio had cooked at nearly every post where his regiment had been stationed and had plenty of experience as a chef.[139]

One of his comrades, Private William Whittington, did not bother to hang around for discharge. The 18-year-old deserted from the hospital that August.[140]

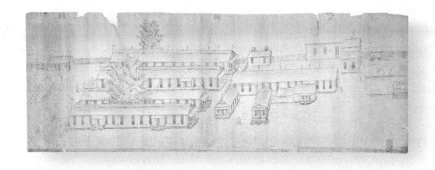

Chapter Eleven

THE GENTLEMAN SURGEON

"The records of the surgeon general's office show that there were 5,532 contract surgeons, or, as they were officially designated, acting assistant surgeons of the U.S.A., who served in the war of the Rebellion."[141]

—Dr. J.T. Nagle, from *Records of the Association of Acting Assistant Surgeons of the United States Army*

The first mention of Dr. George Washington Livesay's work at the Gallipolis hospital was in the spring of 1864. Livesay, a Virginia native, was a Gallipolis physician hired at the hospital as a contract surgeon.142 In an excerpt from her book, *A History of the Army Medical Department: Civil War Medicine, 1861-1865,* Mary Gillette, M.D., wrote that the quality of the Army's contract physicians was important.

"Many routinely staffed general hospitals while others provided help only in emergencies when it was necessary to locate more physicians quickly."

"In the last group were some of the nation's most prominent doctors. When a battle resulted in overwhelming numbers of casualties, those who flocked to the scene might include quacks, cultists, and practitioners of questionable ethics, men who were not under military discipline and who could, therefore, come and go as they liked, taking assignments that pleased them and rejecting all others. They often performed unnecessary operations or wrought havoc as they dug about for bullets."[143]

Dr. Livesay was among the former group of prominent doctors, not at all a "quack." According to family records, he attended the University of Virginia, where he studied chemistry, surgery, medicine, and anatomy and received his medical degree from Columbia University Medical School. He married Elizabeth Lang in Fredonia, New York, her hometown, and they moved to Gallipolis in 1848.[144] In 1862 the Livesays were living in Illinois where he enlisted in Company G of the 60th Illinois Infantry.[145]

Acting Assistant Surgeon George W. Livesay,
60th Illinois Infantry.
Image courtesy Gallia County Historical Society

Livesay was at one point named the Gallipolis Army hospital's Acting Assistant Surgeon. Private, non-commissioned physicians were eligible to serve under contract in that position either in the field or in general hospitals. "This class was very large and embraced in its number some of the most eminent surgeons and physicians of the country," according to *The Medical and Surgical History of the War of the Rebellion (Part III, Volume II, Chapter XIV)*. Gillette estimated that over 5,500 civilian doctors assisted the Army Medical Department during the Civil War.

Livesay was described by one person who knew him as "one of the finest gentlemen in the world. Chesterfieldian in manners, a noble-looking man with a taste for the good, beautiful, and artistic. He was very cultured outside of his profession and a most agreeable companion." A photo of Dr. Livesay taken during his time as Surgeon shows a well-dressed, patrician figure with dark hair and sideburns.[146]

Dr. Livesay built a home for his family known as "Riverby," described as a Federal-style brick home on First Street that overlooks the Ohio River. It is now listed on the National Register of Historic Places.[147]

In the nation's capital, Dorothea Dix used her considerable persuasion and lobbying skills to push for a pay increase for female nurses. At last, in August 1864, the women who served as Army nurses were supplied with food, transportation, housing and 40 cents a day for their work—not a resounding financial victory by any means.[148]

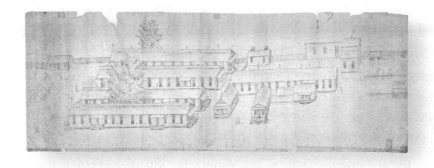

Chapter Twelve

HOSPITALIZED TROOPS TIP THE BALANCE FOR LINCOLN

"This morning, as for some days past, it seems exceedingly probable that this Administration will not be re-elected. Then it will be my duty to so co-operate with the President elect, as to save the Union between the election and the inauguration as he will have secured his election on such ground that he cannot possibly save it afterwards. — A. Lincoln"[149]

—"Blind Memorandum," August 23, 1864,
Abraham Lincoln Papers, Manuscript Division, Library of Congress

1864 was an election year, at least in the remaining Union states, but it was not certain that Americans could vote at all during wartime. It had happened before, during the War of 1812, but the country was far more politically divided during the Civil War, even among Union states.

Nor was Abraham Lincoln's re-election certain. Northerners were weary of the fighting, especially after a series of Union defeats during the summer of 1864. Lincoln was so unsure of his ability to beat Democratic Candidate and former

General of the Army of the Potomac George McClellan that he wrote a memo to his cabinet in which he tried to prepare them for the possibility of his defeat.[150]

But after General William Tecumseh Sherman burned through Atlanta in September, the Lincoln campaign gained some momentum. In order to capitalize on that, Secretary of War Edwin Stanton, a Lincoln supporter, exercised his power to encourage soldiers to vote for the incumbent President.

According to an op-ed written by American Studies Professor and Author Jonathan White, "One of the most notable aspects of the election was the participation of Union soldiers. Nineteen Northern states enacted legislation permitting soldiers to vote away from home."[151]

Union military hospitals had more than the usual reason to furlough soldiers well enough to travel so they could vote. Letters written by Northern Department Medical Director Charles Tripler to Surgeon Lincoln R. Stone show the lengths to which the government in power was willing to go to ensure as many Union soldiers as possible made it to the polls.

"Sir, In reply to yours of October 30th, I have to say that the order to furlough Ohio soldiers to go home to vote includes all soldiers whose homes are in Ohio," Tripler wrote. "P.S. Major General Hooker directs you to furlough all soldiers who wish to vote in West Virginia."[152]

Letters that followed made clear these orders applied to all officers and enlisted men, adding "The Major General Commanding directs me to say that ten days will be a sufficient length of time to grant leave to Officers." The War Department directed Tripler to apprise Stone that he was to extend the furloughs of Indiana soldiers from hospitals "till the 15th November 1864." Memos ordering furloughs for soldiers in hospitals from New Jersey, Wisconsin, Maryland, Pennsylvania, Illinois, and Michigan crossed Stone's desk.

Patients at Gallipolis from New York were not only given furloughs but also rides home. "The Secretary of War directs that all sick and disabled soldiers from the State of New York in hospitals within your command who are unfit for duty but able to go home and who may desire to exercise the elective franchise at the coming election on the Eighth Nov. to be granted furloughs until November Twelfth. Transportation will be furnished by the Q.M. (Quarter Master's) Department to the men as furloughed to their homes and returns."[153]

One cannot look at the results of the 1864 election without thinking the many soldiers who were granted leave from Gallipolis and other Army hospitals had an impact in re-electing President Lincoln, who won both the electoral votes—212, compared to McClellan's 21—and the popular vote, beating McClellan fifty-five percent to forty-five percent. According to White, Lincoln won 78 percent of the soldier vote.

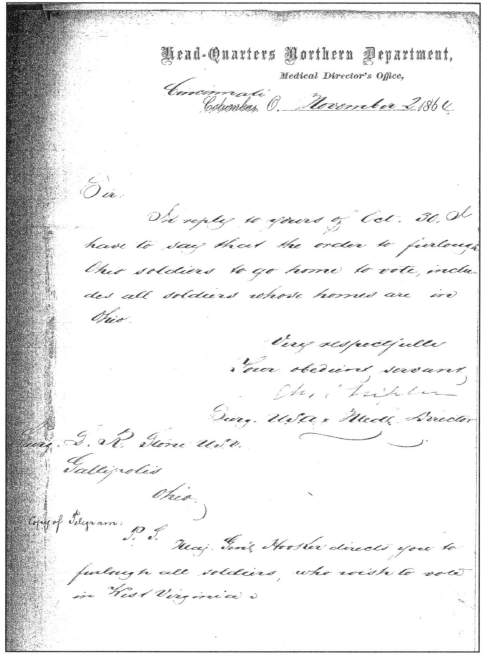

Correspondence to Surgeon Lincoln R. Stone, November 1864.
National Archives

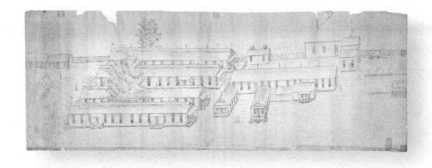

Chapter Thirteen

A WAR WIDOW FINDS HOSPITAL WORK

"David W. Cherrington, Co. H, 2nd Reg't West Virginia Cavalry.
Wounded in action Sept. 22, 1864 at Fisher Hill, Va. Leg amputated.
Discharged March 29, 1865 by reason of expiration of
service, Gallipolis Hospital."[154]

—Company H Muster-out Roll Card

Gallia County-born Gallipolis native David Cherrington was 28 when he enlisted in Company H of the 2nd West Virginia Cavalry. At five feet, eight and a half inches tall, he was the height of an average Civil War soldier. The blue-eyed, light-haired farmer was mustered in as a bugler.[155]

His regiment saw action at Fisher's Hill, near Strasburg, Virginia, in September 1864, and he was wounded in the right leg. He was taken to the U.S. Army General Hospital at Clarysville, Maryland, where surgeons amputated his leg. After a period of healing, Cherrington wrote to the Adjutant General, Department of West Virginia, asking if he might be transferred to the hospital at Gallipolis, "… in order that I may be where I can receive the visits of my friends." His request was granted and Cherrington arrived at the U.S. Army General Hospital at Gallipolis in December. Dr. Stone examined the musician and determined that he was permanently disabled upon admission.[156]

David W. Cherrington bed card, Clarysville Civil War Hospital
Digital Collection, West Virginia & Regional History Center,
West Virginia University, Morgantown, West Virginia.

In early 1865, Dr. Stone issued a fresh copy of Rules and Regulations for the Government of the U.S.A. General Hospital, Gallipolis, Ohio, and it gives an excellent overview of an average day at the hospital:

"The following calls will be observed until further orders:
Reveille, 6 ½ a.m.
Breakfast, 7 a.m.
Fatigue-call, 8 a.m.
Surgeon's-call, 9 a.m.
Recall from light-duty, 11 ½ a.m.
Dinner-call, 12 p.m.

Fatigue-call, 1 p.m.

Recall, 3 ½ p.m.

Surgeon's evening call, 4 p.m.

Supper, 5 p.m.

Tattoo, 8 ½ p.m.

Taps, 9 p.m.

Church calls, Sunday 2 ½ & 6 p.m.; Wednesdays, at 6 p.m."[157]

RULES AND REGULATIONS
For the Government of the U. S. A. General Hospital,
GALLIPOLIS, OHIO.

1. No patient or attendant will be allowed to leave the Hospital without permission of the Surgeon in charge, and with a pass signed by the Officer of the Day. Before leaving the Hospital on his pass, each patient will deliver his bed-card to the clerk who registers the pass from whom he will receive it again on his return. Passes will be issued between 10 o'clock A. M., and 12 o'clock, M; patients will be recommended for passes by the Attending Surgeon; nurses and cooks by the Steward. Passes for attendants will be from 1 to 3 o'clock, P. M.

2. No smoking, swearing or spitting on the floor, will be allowed in the wards.

3. The beds will be made every morning by the attendants, (oftener if necessary:) patients able to do so, however, will make their own beds.

4. Patients are not allowed to occupy the beds without undressing, or to sit or lounge upon them; caps and hats are not to be worn in the wards; they are to be put in the ward clothes room.

5. Every patient who is able, will wash his face and hands and clean his shoes at least every morning; those unable to do this will have it done for them by the attendants. All patients on their entrance to the Hospital, whose condition does not forbid it, will take a bath.

6. At sick-call, every patient will repair immediately to his ward and remain at his bed until visited by the Surgeon.

7. Convalescents able to do light duty will be detailed for such work as they can perform. The list of these men will be furnished daily by the Attending Surgeon. At fatigue-call, the Head-nurses will collect them and turn them over to the Chief-Steward, who will assign them to duty under a competent non-commissioned officer; the passes for light-duty men will be from 4 to 6 o'clock, P. M.

8. All lights in the Hospital must be extinguished at taps, except those necessary.

9. No persons will be allowed to enter the Hospital without special permission from the Surgeon in charge, or the Officer of the Day, except on Sundays, Mondays, Wednesdays and Fridays, between the hours of 3 and 5 o'clock, P. M.

10. No provisions or spirituous liquors of any kind shall be brought within the Hospital without permission of the Medical Officer of the Day.

11. Patients will give prompt obedience to the Stewards, Ward-Master and Nurses in all lawful demands.

The following CALLS, will be observed until further orders.

Reveille,	6 1-2 A. M.	Fatigue-call,	1	P. M.
Breakfast,	7 "	Recall,	3 1-2 "
Fatigue-call,	8 "	Surgeon's evening call,	4 "
Surgeon's-call,	9 "	Supper,	5 "
Recall from light-duty,	11 1-2 "	Tattoo,	8 1-2 "
Dinner-call,	12 "	Taps,	9 "

Church calls, Sunday, 2 1-2 & 6 p. m.; Wednesdays, at 6 p. m.

Lincoln R. Stone,

December 12th, 1864.   SURGEON U. S. VOL's., IN CHARGE OF HOSPITAL.

Rules & Regulations for the U.S. Army General Hospital, Gallipolis, Ohio.
Courtesy of Terry Lowry

In early March, Surgeon Stone wrote to the Medical Director of the Department of West Virginia Surgeon A.B. Campbell, asking for permission to hire Mrs. Elizabeth J. White. "She is a wife of a soldier killed in action during the past summer, and is I think a worthy person. I consider it quite necessary that some woman should be employed in such capacity with a view of having charge of the extra and light diet kitchen and know no one so capable as she."[158]

Elizabeth's husband Lucien had been a Corporal in the 34th Ohio Infantry. He died in October 1864 in Philadelphia, leaving Elizabeth and her three-year-old daughter Frances behind. Dr. George Livesay remembered seeing Elizabeth in the hospital kitchen with Frances playing nearby. "... I was employed as an assistant surgeon in the U.S. General Hospital located at Gallipolis during the war, and know that said Elizabeth J. Fulton (then White) was in the hospital as an employee," he explained in a letter written on Elizabeth's behalf when she later applied for pension benefits for her daughter. "She had with her at the time a child which she alleges is the same as the one now produced."[159]

Elizabeth would have referred to a poster on the hospital kitchen wall to choose and prepare the multiple types of diets necessary for different patients. The United States Army Diet Table for General Hospitals listed the foods and amounts for a full diet, half diet, chicken diet, low diet, milk diet and a beef-tea diet. Extra diets included such items as beefsteak, mutton chops, fish, and veal. Extra drinks covered everything from lemonade and barley water, to "medicinal" wine, ale, brandy, and whiskey.[160]

As patient numbers decreased later that month, Steward Charles Bosworth placed an ad in the *Gallipolis Journal:* "For Sale at the U.S. Gen. Hospital at Gallipolis, 50 Iron Bunks, Wrought and Strap Iron. 2 Stoves. 4 kettles, 30 gallons each. Can be seen at any time, and disposed of at private sale."[161]

On March 20th, David Cherrington's term of military service expired. Dr. Stone signed his Certificate of Discharge Due to Disability and he soon received an artificial leg, courtesy of the U.S. Government.[162]

Around that same time, a New York soldier was admitted to the hospital, suffering from chronic diarrhea, a common wartime ailment among soldiers. 29-year-old Robert Armstrong, a private in the 15th New York Cavalry, had been sick for several months and was "very much emaciated," according to a report Dr. Stone wrote about his case. Stone prescribed "Ipecacuanha eight grains, persulphate of iron fifteen grains, catechu fifteen grains, opium five grains; make eight powders. Take one every two hours. Milk diet."

By March 30th, Armstrong was improving. Stone wrote: "Is cheerful and decidedly improving; tongue furred; stomach somewhat irritable. Continue the powders ordered yesterday, every three hours, and give five grains of calomel."

"March 31st: Toward evening, today, the patient who had been writing home and seemed very much depressed, was allowed a drink of brandy. Subsequently he contrived to get at the brandy bottle and drank to intoxication. He died the next morning, April 1st, at 4:00 a.m."[163]

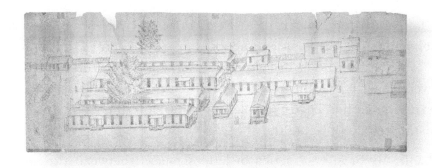

Chapter Fourteen

THE CURTAIN
COMES DOWN

"Resolved, That Friday next be observed as recommended: that the exercises commence by the ringing of all the bells in the city at 6 o'clock A.M., that the clergymen and congregations of the several churches, observe the day by suitable religious services in their respective churches at 10 1/2 o'clock A.M. That a salute of 100 guns be fired at 12 P.M.; that the citizens meet at the Court House at 2 P.M. for public addresses; that all the bells be again rung at 6 o'clock P.M., and a salute of 36 guns be then fired; that a grand torch light procession of all the military, different orders, societies, and citizens, generally, be formed at 7 1/2 P.M. at the corner of Second and Court streets, and then march through the principal streets of the city.

Resolved, That the citizens be, and they are hereby recommended to suspend all business, close their business houses, and join in the jubilee."[164]

—Minutes of citizen's meeting, Mayor's Office,
April 12, 1865, *Gallipolis Journal*

Lieutenant General Ulysses S. Grant's troops and horses had been mired in Virginia—literally and figuratively, as heavy snows gave way to spring rains, creating rough, muddy conditions that hampered travel—in late March and into April. General Philip Sheridan had burned through the Shenandoah Valley the previous fall, and Union advances at Five Forks and Petersburg ushered in the fall of Richmond. The Siege of Petersburg, ten months on at that point, had led to mass Confederate soldier desertions but also wore on the North's nerves as citizens were eager for Grant to defeat the rebels. General Robert E. Lee's Army of Northern Virginia had begun the siege with 60,000 troops; by April, there were only an estimated 20,000-22,000.[165]

On April 9th, 1865, after a series of letters passed between the generals, Lee agreed to meet Grant at Appomattox Courthouse to discuss the terms that would be acceptable for the South's surrender. At two separate tables in a house owned by the McLean family, the generals agreed to terms which Grant wrote out in a letter addressed to Lee. It read, in part:

> "The officers to give their individual paroles not to take up arms against the Government of the United States until properly exchanged, and each company or regimental commander sign a like parole for the men of their commands. The arms, artillery, and public property to be parked and stacked, and turned over to the officer appointed by me to receive them. This will not embrace the side-arms of the officers, nor their private horses or baggage. This done, each officer and man will be allowed to return to their homes, not to be disturbed by United States authority so long as they observe their paroles and the laws in force where they may reside."[166]

The telegram Grant subsequently sent to Secretary of War Edwin M. Stanton was published in the *Gallipolis Journal*:

> "Headq'rs Army of U.S., April 9—4:30 p.m.
>
> To E.M. Stanton, Sec'y of War
>
> General Lee surrendered the Army of Northern Virginia this afternoon, upon the terms proposed by myself. The accompanying additional correspondence will show the condition fully."
>
> (Signed) U.S. Grant, Lieutenant General[167]

Soon after the news reached Gallipolis, church bells rang and fireworks burst in the night sky. The following day, a detachment of Lee's army numbering 110 steamed into Gallipolis on board the General Meigs. They were, according to a news report, deserters who had not heard about Lee's surrender until they reached southeastern Ohio.

By this time, ownership of the *Journal* had changed hands. Harper had sold the newspaper to R.L. Stewart, who in the April 13th issue opined about Lee's surrender and how the other C.S.A. generals would no doubt give up the fight as well:

> "Their divisions will melt away like snow before the summer sun when they once learn that Lee is no longer dictator of the Confederacy, and that Jeff Davis and his cabinet are skulking through by-roads and out of the way places, in order to escape their well merited doom."[168]

> At the hospital, the surgeons prepared to receive 800 patients from other Army hospitals who were being moved to make room for the wounded from the Richmond campaign. The incoming patients stretched the hospital's indoor capacity, there being only 350 beds in the wards. "About 70 tents have already been set up, and ample accommodations are being made for our gallant boys, who we trust may soon be allowed to return to their homes."[169]

After all the bloodshed on both sides during the war, there would, by the end of that week, be another episode of violence that would rock the entire world.

ASSASSINATION OF PRESIDENT LINCOLN!!!

He is Shot Through the Head While in the Theater

Wound Pronounced Mortal!

Cleveland Morning Leader, Saturday, April 15, 1865

An entry in First Lieutenant Jacob Wickerham's diary reflected the shock waves that crashed through Union regiments in mid-April 1865 following President Lincoln's assassination.

> "This morning when we wer making all preparations to rejoice over the Great victory of the past five days the 'awful news' flashed across the wires of the fiendish assassination of our Noble and magnimous President Abraham Lincoln and Mr. Seward Stabbed in his dying bed according to flying accounts for the first time for many months I could shed tears freely and Oh, when looking at the war worn Soldiers who Came out to rejoice and at Once they reversed their arms muffled the drums the flags wer draped in mourning and all seemed to be sad."[170]

Hours before the Lincolns left the White House for Ford's Theatre, Hospital Chaplain Reverend Henry Stevens had spoken at the courthouse during a

Gallipolis celebration of the war's end. Stevens was planning on opening a hospital school for patients and had put out a request to the community for schoolbooks not being used by children in the area.

An eyewitness identified as Miss Harris, who was seated in the President's box at the theater, relayed these details of the assassination, as reported in a special dispatch to the *Cincinnati Gazette:*

> "Nearly an hour before the commission of the deed, the assassin came to the door of the box and looked in, to take a survey of the position of its occupants. Supposing it to be either a mistake or the exercise of an impertinent curiosity, this circumstance, at the time, attracted little attention.
>
> Upon his entering the box again, however, Major Rathbone arose and asked the intruder his business. He pushed past him without reply, and placed his pistol close to the back of the President's head, and actually in contact with it, as Miss Harris thinks, and fired.
>
> He then instantly sprang upon the cushioned bannister of the box, where he made a backward plunge with his knife, aimed at the face or breast of Mr. Lincoln. Maj. Rathbone, springing forward to protect the President, received the stab in his arm. The murderer then jumped upon the stage and effected his escape."[171]

Hospital records and correspondence from the period of time after Lincoln's assassination are silent as to how the surgeons, staff and patients reacted to the news of the President's death, although one can speculate with little doubt that hearts were heavy with grief. Work continued, though. Paperwork dated April 15th, 1865 flowed as always from the Medical Directors' offices to Dr. Stone and from his desk back to theirs, as well as orders from Washington.

Meanwhile, Dr. Bell had shipped off to Madison, Indiana, to help the staff shutter the U.S. Army hospital there as wards emptied. "It was very extensive, numbering 57 wards and at one time, 3,300 patients," the *Journal* reported. "Dr. Bell by his energy and kind attention to the soldiers under his charge was presented with a splendid tea set, including $100 worth of silver spoons as a testimonial of their esteem."[172]

Bell put an ad in the newspaper upon his return from Indiana: "Dr. James R. Bell tenders his professional services to the citizens of Gallipolis and vicinity."[173] He would practice medicine in Gallipolis for many years to come.

An Army medical inspector chastised Surgeon Stone for not providing him with Invoices of Inspection of Condemned Supplies of Medical and Hospital Items. Lieutenant Colonel George W. Stipp directed Stone to forward the needed papers, without delay. Never mind that Dr. Stone was busy running the hospital, treating patients or discharging them for disability and under orders to allow muster out of those no longer in need of medical care. He had little time for less urgent matters like condemned property.[174]

Stone was annoyed with Stipp for another reason as well. He wrote to Colonel Alexander Dougherty, Medical Director for the Department of West Virginia, questioning how Stipp was qualified to inspect his hospital for property or anything else. "I have the honor to report that Lieut. Col. G.W. Stipp, Medical Inspector U.S.A. Northern Department, visited this hospital a day or so ago claiming that it was in his inspection department," he wrote in early June. "I objected on the ground that the hospital was in the Dept. of W. Va. He inspected and recommended for condemnation a few articles of hospital property, but confined himself to that duty alone... He also gives me in communication of today directions in regard to discharge my soldiers, and on these points, I would respectfully request to be informed what course to pursue under the circumstances."[175]

At the end of warfare, the hospital began winding down. Surgeons J.C. Rathburn, Levi Lathrop, and George W. Livesay were nearing the ends of their contracts, and Medical Director Dougherty peppered Stone with questions about which acting assistant surgeons, civilian nurses, cooks and employees, could be dropped or their services supplied by enlisted men of the Veterans Reserve Corps (formerly Invalid Corps) and convalescents. Ohio Governor Brough announced that all Ohio soldiers in Departments of the East, Pennsylvania, Washington "and the middle department" would be transferred to the state's U.S. Army hospitals if they were not eligible to be mustered out or were unfit for duty for 30 days.

Dr. Stone received this letter from Col. Dougherty in early June:

> "Sir,
>
> Nothing has been heard from the Surgeon General: you will therefore proceed to break up the Hospital under your charge without further delay, in accordance with instructions from this office under date of May 25th, 1865."[176]

In the June 22nd issue of the local newspaper, this item appeared: "The hospital at this post may be said to have 'played out.' The boys are all discharged and at home or transferred to Grafton [West Virginia Army Hospital], quite as much to their satisfaction as the relief of our citizens."[177]

But the hospital remained open for a time after that. A report published on August 24th stated that government buildings on the Public Square, which had served as the supply depot, and on hospital grounds were not yet sold. There are references to poor families from other states who were possibly fed and treated at the hospital, while there were still a dwindling number of soldiers and staff at the post.[178]

An article published on October 26th claimed the hospital had been unused for nearly four months, which means it closed for good sometime in July, which aligns with information given on the hospital's Ohio Historical Marker, which stands at the site today. "Great complaints are made by our citizens, relative to the delay in removing the Government buildings from our Public Square and other parts of town," the article read.[179] It seems the townspeople wanted to dispose of any remnants of the war quickly, as well as the awful memories of it.

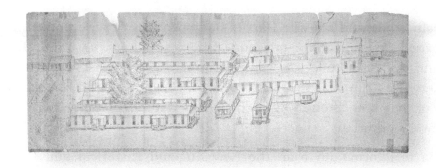

Chapter Fifteen

THE WORK THAT KNITTED HEART TO HEART AND SOUL TO SOUL

"That was the work that knitted heart to heart and soul to soul, for we worked for the soldier boy in blue. Our men were fighting for principle. I had no husband to go, but others had and they were loved ones. I had no son to go in this great work so I went myself, it was all I could do."[180]

—from a speech delivered by Hannah Maxon at a
national Woman's Relief Corps meeting

Captain John C. Gerard, assistant quartermaster of the post, sold the buildings of the Gallipolis United States Army General Hospital on Tuesday, April 12th, 1866. A *Journal* ad detailed the government sale. "22 hospital buildings," along with one steam engine and boiler, one copper pump, two water tanks, five office chairs, one stove and a quantity of lead and iron pipe were auctioned off.[181]

Only 18 buildings were purchased, however. Seven months after the sale, hospital grounds landowner Stephen Barlow put it all up for sale. He offered 26 acres with four buildings with cisterns, one well and more. Those ads ran in the *Journal* through January 1867.

Dr. Lincoln Stone and his wife Harriet had spent the first seventeen months of their married life living on the grounds of the hospital. In July 1865, the hospital closed and Surgeon Stone was sent to Harpers Ferry, West Virginia, where he briefly served as Surgeon in Charge of a U.S. Army General Hospital there. In October of that year, Stone was promoted to Lieutenant Colonel by Brevet "for faithful and meritorious services."[182]

According to information from the New England Historical and Genealogical Society, the couple's first child, Laura, was born on August 23, 1865, in Harpers Ferry. The Stones had four more children, including a set of twins, all boys, all born in Newton, Massachusetts between 1869 and 1873.

After mustering out from the U.S. Volunteers Medical Department, Lincoln Stone returned to private practice in Newton where he also contributed to local government, sitting on the town's education board in the 1880s and serving as his local medical society's librarian. He lived to be almost 100 years old and died May 27, 1931.[183]

Dr. Francis Salter was Surgeon in Charge at Chattanooga Army Hospital Number One in 1864. During his time in Tennessee, he advocated on behalf of the first female War Department Surgeon, Dr. Mary C. Walker. A graduate of Syracuse (NY) Medical College, Surgeon Walker had to fight for the right to treat soldiers and spent the early war years working as a volunteer; she was eventually given the right to be paid by the War Department. At Chattanooga she asked Surgeon Salter for a position as an assistant surgeon. Salter first gave her charge of the measles ward, where all the patients recovered under her treatment. He then appointed her to be a ward inspector, effectively giving her a supervisory role over the hospital's assistant surgeons.[184]

Salter was then named Surgeon, U.S. Volunteers, of the Fourth U.S. Cavalry, whose troops engaged in campaigns in Alabama and Georgia for nearly a month in spring 1865. He was promoted to Brevet Lieutenant Colonel "for meritorious and efficient discharge of his duties in caring for the sick and wounded throughout the campaign."[185]

The 1870 Ohio Census shows Salter's wife Mary Jane as head of her household, no husband listed, living with her five sons and daughter in Circleville, Ohio.[186] But Surgeon Francis Salter was living in Washington, D.C. in 1870—with his wife Edna Powell McDonald Salter.[187]

The plot thickens around Mary Jane and Francis' marital status. Surgeon Salter's descendant Nicole Hixon does not believe the Salters ever divorced. "From my understanding, she always believed that he had died in the Civil War," Nicole wrote in an email. "Our family cemetery plot was started by Mary, and her headstone lists her as wife of Dr. Francis Salter."[188]

As of this writing, no divorce documentation for the Salters has been found. Despite the fact that Mary Jane's headstone at Forest Cemetery in Circleville, Ohio, is engraved with "Wife of Dr. F. Salter," there is a November 18, 1866, marriage record for Francis Salter and Edna Powell McDonald.[189] They wed in Tennessee and had two children. They moved to Washington, D.C., where he worked as a U.S. Pension Bureau medical referee. Edna died in 1878, and Francis died the following year at the age of 48. Both are buried at Flint Hill Cemetery in Oakton, Virginia.[190] Mary Jane outlived them both, dying February 28th, 1897.[191]

Dr. James Bell continued treating the citizens in and around Gallipolis. He and his wife Sara had two children, Ella, born in 1858, and Oscar, born four years after the war ended. Oscar grew up to be a doctor like his father. At some point, the Bells moved to Springfield, Ohio, where Hannah visited them in 1899.[192] "With the exception of Mrs. Bell, who has been an invalid for nearly two years, unable to walk, [Hannah] reports all the Gallipolis colony there well."[193]

After Sara's death in 1901, Dr. Bell lived with Oscar in Dayton, Ohio.[194] He was eventually admitted to the U.S. National Home for Disabled Volunteer Soldiers in that city. He was 86 years old when admitted, and still receiving an Army pension, which he earned with the help of 7th OVI comrade Charles C. Bosworth.[195]

Bosworth wrote a letter to the U.S. House of Representatives Committee on Invalid Pensions in 1888, certifying that Bell's neuralgia attack at Charleston, Virginia, was diagnosed by Dr. Salter, that it debilitated him for the rest of his life, and that he himself helped nurse Bell back to health.[196] James Ross Bell died in 1910 and is buried at Massie Creek Cemetery in Greene County, Ohio. In 1910, Bosworth and his wife Sarah and son Ernest were living in Ringgold County, Iowa, and he was listed as a farmer.[197] He died in December 1920.

Hospital Steward Corporal Joseph Lunbeck headed west after the war. In 1870, he and Agnes lived in Saline County, Missouri, with their children Elmer, Rowena and Ernest. They eventually had two more sons, and Joseph opened a farming equipment and hardware store next to their home in Malta Bend, Missouri while Agnes operated a millinery business on their property.[198] The family later moved to Emporia, Kansas, and then on to Denver, where two of their sons worked as salesmen. Joseph died in April 1908 at 71. He and Agnes are buried at Grandview Cemetery in Chillicothe.[199]

After he returned to private practice in Gallipolis, Dr. George W. Livesay became a medical examiner for the Charter Oak Life Insurance Company.[200] He then partnered with Dr. William C.H. Needham, who moved from Massachusetts to Gallipolis, and they opened a practice on Front Street.[201] Livesay then sold the practice to Needham, and he and his family left Gallipolis, moving to Chicago, in the summer of 1870.

The Livesays' time in Chicago was cut short by the great fire of 1871 and the family returned to Ohio afterwards. George, or "Wash" as he was called, began doctoring in Ironton, Ohio. His wife Elizabeth died before the turn of the century; he lived until 1900, died at age 75, and is buried at Woodland Cemetery in Ironton.[202] The Livesay home, Riverby, is today home to Gallipolis' French Art Colony, a multi-arts center open to the public, and the Riverby Theatre Guild.[203]

Riverby, now home to the French Art Colony in Gallipolis, Ohio.
Courtesy of the French Art Colony.

The teacher who stepped forward for duty in the beginning of the Civil War continued to serve her community and country after war's end. Hannah Maxon returned to teaching once again at Union School, and except for taking a job in Springfield, Ohio for three years, she taught in Gallia County schools for over 45 years, primarily at Union, Mill Creek and Grant Schools.[204]

She was known as an effective disciplinarian in the classroom and a teacher who applied practical, sometimes unorthodox, tactics to intractable problems. When schoolchildren contracted head lice, "Miss Hannah Maxon did not waste time with notes home to parents, she herded the suspects into the school hall and dosed their heads liberally with kerosene. That killed the bugs quickly and there was little trouble (*Gallipolis Daily Tribune*)."[205]

There is more than sufficient evidence that many students revered her, even after they left her classroom. On the fortieth anniversary of her teaching (1902), she hosted a reception at Gallia Academy (her alma mater) for three generations of her students. An article in *The Dayton Herald* stated that "*Miss Maxon has kept a record of all her school years and the names of more than 1,100 pupils are thereon. At the close of the exercises, she was presented with a diamond ring and pin by her scholars.*"[206] Decades later, former students' obituaries often mentioned Miss Maxon as a huge influence in their lives.

Her impact on the entire local school system was notable. The writer of a 1950 *Gallia Times* column claims that "school buildings in the city were named [after Presidents] Washington, Lincoln, Grant, Garfield and Douglas upon suggestion of Miss Hannah Maxon long after the close of the Civil War."[207]

She cared for her aging mother until her death in 1899, after which Hannah devoted more time to local and national organizations. As years went on, she became active in the temperance movement. "Impressed by the ravages of intemperance, she was long active in doing a woman's full share toward combating them," wrote a *Tribune* editor. "No blustering or abusive adherent of evil could daunt her spirit for even a moment. She launched many a telling shaft of stinging truth full in the faces of wicked men, and did it when many men, unable to face the hostility of powerful influences controlled by lawless elements, dodged and retired from the conflict."[208]

Hannah volunteered enthusiastically for post-war activities that honored Union dead and provided charitable support to widows and orphans left behind. She and her school threw a benefit for a U.S. Army veteran who had been denied his pension despite being wounded in the war, and the funds helped him pay his bills.[209]

Each Decoration Day and Memorial Day, Hannah enlisted local children to help her place flowers on soldier graves at Pine Street Cemetery. Some residents did not believe Confederate soldiers' graves ought to be decorated along with Union ones. Although some in the community objected, Hannah and her helpers placed flowers on Southern soldiers' graves as well.[210] All but four of the 80 Confederate graves are labeled Unknown Soldiers. The four identified Rebels buried there all died at the U.S. Army General Hospital—William Z. Wickline, Robert J. Thrasher, James H. McKinney, and Adam S. Rader. They were privates of the 22nd Virginia Infantry, all taken as prisoners of war at the May 1862 Battle of Lewisburg and brought to Gallipolis.[211]

Sketch of Hannah Utley Maxon, which appeared in the *National Tribune*, a newspaper for Civil War Veterans, in 1895.

Hannah rose through the ranks of the state and national chapters of the Women's Relief Corps (W.R.C.), an auxiliary group to the Grand Army of the Republic, the preeminent Civil War veterans' organization that formed after the war. Known as a witty and eloquent speaker, she became Department President of the Ohio W.R.C., and became National Chaplain in 1904, an office she held until her death. At that time, there were nearly 150,000 members nationwide. She traveled across the country to W.R.C. conventions, speaking and offering invocations, and served as an Inspector of the various chapters.[212]

The National Tribune (Washington, D.C.) profiled Hannah in a May 1895 issue: "She is a veritable Florence Nightingale with a heart overflowing with Christian love and sympathy, yet firm and inflexible in right, and well-fitted to perform with dignity and honor the high duty of Department President."[213]

One of her former pupils relayed this anecdote about Hannah's W.R.C. chaplaincy to a Gallipolis newspaper:

> "The [W.R.C.] was in session, if I remember correctly, in Cleveland, Ohio, when the terrible deed of the assassination of President McKinley took place. The intelligence was brought to the large assembly while in the midst of their work. The house seemed paralyzed. For an instant no word was uttered. Hannah Maxon, sitting upon the platform with other officials, arose, walked to the front of the stage as if impelled by a great spiritual impulse, and said in her clear, penetrating voice 'Let us pray,' and such a prayer I never heard uttered before or since, said my informant, the assembly were in tears. I think it was this incident that cause Miss Maxon from that time till her death to be chosen as the National Chaplain of the Woman's Relief Corps."[214]

She was introduced on stage at one of the national W.R.C. conventions by Annie Wittenmyer, the high-profile U.S. Christian Commission representative who created hospital special diet kitchens. Wittenmyer said: "Hannah Maxon of Ohio. She did not go to the hospital, it came to her." Hannah addressed the audience with humility and grace. "I was under the supervision of Miss Dix. Sisters mine, we are united in heart. May we be more devoted than ever to that flag, the one flag of these United States. There is no other association that insists on the study of patriotism and if we do not teach patriotism we are not fulfilling our pledge to our country, ourselves and our God."[215]

Along with other female U.S. Army nurses, the federal government eventually rewarded Hannah's nursing. In August 1907, the headline in Gallipolis read "Hannah Maxon Gets Pension."

> "A pension plum has come to our fellow townswoman, Miss Hannah V. [sic] Maxon of $414.40 per year. She gets it as an army nurse, who cared for the wounded boys in blue from '61 to '65. This will be glad news to hundreds whom she has taught in our public schools and who grew into useful citizens under her guidance."[216]

Hannah Utley Maxon died in her home, just down the street from where she was born, on May 26, 1910, at age 69. The cause of death was bladder cancer and her death certificate was signed by the first woman physician in Gallipolis, Dr. Ella G. Lupton.[217] Thanks to an Act of Congress supported by the National Association of Army Nurses of the Civil War, Hannah was entitled to burial in a National Cemetery alongside those who fought. She was laid to rest at Pine Street Cemetery in Gallipolis.[218]

> "It was fitting that this woman should be buried as she was, with military honors and that she should be saluted in her casket by the Grand Army of the Republic. As she passes out from among us to the quiet of the earth, he is indeed unheeding who does not yield to her memory the tribute due her active and useful life as a teacher, reformer, patriot, and brave antagonist of wrongdoing."
>
> —*Gallipolis Daily Tribune,* May 31, 1910

Appendix A

Surgeons of the U.S. Army General Hospital, Gallipolis, Ohio

Acting Assistant Surgeon C.D. Arnold, U.S.A.

Acting Assistant Surgeon John Quincy Adams Banta, U.S.A.

Assistant Surgeon, Surgeon Charles A. Barlow (also known as Augustus C. Barlow), 4th West Virginia Infantry, 8th West Virginia Infantry, 47th Ohio Infantry, 62 Ohio Infantry

Acting Assistant Surgeon, Surgeon James Ross Bell, 7th Ohio Infantry

Surgeon John Seth Combs, 153rd Infantry Ohio National Guard

Assistant Surgeon Frederick Augustus Cromley, U.S.A.

Surgeon Oliver E. Davis, 119th Ohio Infantry

Surgeon Jonas Frank Gabriel, 11th Ohio Infantry

Assistant Surgeon, Surgeon Perrin Gardner, 1st West Virginia Cavalry

Surgeon John E. Herbst, U.S.A.

Assistant Surgeon Bradford F. Holcombe, 34th & 36th Ohio Infantry

Assistant Surgeon James Johnston, 116th & 141st Ohio Infantry

Hospital Steward, Acting Assistant Surgeon Levi B. Lathrop, 101st Ohio Infantry & 131st Ohio Infantry National Guard

Assistant Surgeon, Surgeon John Williams Lawton, U.S. Volunteers & 2nd Connecticut Heavy Artillery

Contract Surgeon David Lewis

Acting Assistant Surgeon, Contract Surgeon George W. Livesay, U.S.A. & 60th Illinois Infantry

Assistant Surgeon, Surgeon William Waddell Mills, 18th Ohio Infantry

Assistant Surgeon, Surgeon John Morgan, 32nd Ohio Infantry, 172nd Infantry Ohio National Guard, & 2nd Ohio Heavy Artillery

Assistant Surgeon, Surgeon Edward B. Mosher, 172nd Ohio National Guard

Surgeon David Noble, 60th Ohio Infantry

Acting Assistant Surgeon, Surgeon, Contract Surgeon William H. Phillips, 118th Ohio Infantry

Acting Assistant Surgeon, Contract Surgeon James C. Rathburn, U.S.A.

Surgeon James Dickey Robison, U.S.A. & 16th Ohio Infantry

Assistant Surgeon James H. Rouse, 8th West Virginia Mounted Infantry & 7th West Virginia Cavalry

Acting Assistant Surgeon James B. Ruttan, U.S.A.

Assistant Surgeon, Surgeon Francis Salter, U.S.A. & 7th Ohio Infantry

Assistant Surgeon, Surgeon Nelson Banks Sisson, 92nd Ohio Infantry

Surgeon Lincoln Ripley Stone, U.S. Volunteers & 2nd Massachusetts Infantry & 54th Massachusetts, United States Colored Troops

Assistant Surgeon & 1st Lieutenant George Wyman, 172nd and 173rd Ohio Infantry

Assistant Surgeon Bradford F. Holcombe.
Photo courtesy of Nona Press. Image credit: Joe Anidjar.

Assistant Surgeon James Johnston. *Gallipolis Daily Tribune.*

Assistant Surgeon James H. Rouse. Image courtesy of Steve Cunningham.

APPENDIX B

Staff of the U.S. Army General Hospital, Gallipolis, Ohio

Matron Estaline Allen

William Augustus

Eliza Bishol

Chaplain Charles Morris Blake, U.S.A., 13th Missouri Infantry & 3rd United States Colored Troops

Clerk Sebastian Bolway, Adjutant General's Office (Union Regular Army)

Hospital Steward/Druggist/Wardmaster Charles C. Bosworth, 7th Ohio Infantry

Matron Jane Brown

Matron Mary Brown

Matron Mary Bryant

Matron Margaret Butterfield

Matron Susan Callaway

Assistant Druggist William J. Long. Gallia County Historical Society.

Laundress Eliza Chapman

Matron Lorinda Chapman

Matron Tamer Clinger

Matron Jane Colley

Matron Martha Colley

Matron Lucy Colly

Matron Mary O. Conley

Matron Pheby Conrod

Matron Mary Cook

Druggist Fred Cromley

E. Daly

Matron C. Darnell

Matron Margret Davis

Matron Rachel Davis

Matron Sarah Davis

Matron Cornelia Dean

Matron Julia Ann Dean

Hospital Steward John R. Downer, 172nd Ohio Infantry National Guard

Matron Jane Duffy

Hospital Steward Patrick Duffy, U.S.A.

Matron Susan Duket

Matron Fanny Eve

Catharine Farnett

Matron Mary Farrall

Jane Frazer

Wardmaster William F. Ridgely. Gallia County Historical Society.

Hospital Steward William French, Captain Smith's Ohio Trumbull Guards

Matron Ann E. Frisbee

Matron Rachel Fulton, 37th Iowa Infantry

Matron Eliza Garrett

Mary Glasby

Matron Jane Goshorn

Matron & Laundress Josephine Gregory

Clerk Gardner Griswold, 108th New York Infantry, 44th U.S. Infantry (Regular Army), 11th Veteran Reserve Corps and Company 21, 2nd Battalion Veteran Reserve Corps

Clerk H.A. Grose

E.C. Haines

Matron Cordelia Haines/Hayne/ Haynes

Matron Francis Haines/Haynes

Matron Elizabeth Halley

Matron Jane Halley

Matron Margret Halley

Matron Catherine Harper

Matron & Laundress Sarah Heaton

Matron Sarah Hill, Jr.

Matron Francis Jackson

Julia Johnson

Reuben Johnson

Matron Betsey Jones

Matron Jane Jones

Matron Lucy Jones

Matron Mary Jones

Sarah Jones

Clerk James W. Searles. Gallia County Historical Society

Matron Susan Jones

Mary Kelley

Matron & Laundress Susan Ketcher

Steward Joseph Max Koenig, U.S.A.

Matron Ellen Lee

Clerk Robert H.T. Leipold, 6th Pennsylvania Cavalry

Matron Catharine Lester

Matron Jane Lewis

Matron & Nurse Susan Lewis

Assistant Druggist William J. Long, 98th Ohio Infantry & 2nd Battalion Veteran Reserve Corps

Hospital Steward Cpl. Joseph R. Lunbeck, U.S.A. and 26th Ohio Infantry

Matron Alvira Lyons

Matron L. Marshall

Matron Elvyra Masser

Matron Jane McCafferty

Matron Jane McCoy

Matron C. McMakin

Matron Sarah J. McQuaid

Matron Lucinda Mercer/Messer

Woodson Mitchell, 44th United States Colored Troops

Matron Lucy Morris

Matron Eliza Murphy

Matron Manerva/Minerva Murphy

Matron Elizabeth Nidick

Matron Bridget O'Brian/O'Brien

Matron Margaret O'Harra/O'Harry

Evaline Page

Matron Mary Ann Parmley

Maron Mary Ann Pasco

Matron Fanny Peters

Matron Nancy Phelps

Matron Mary Polley/Polly

Matron & Nurse Margaret Randal

Matron & Nurse Mary Randal

Matron & Nurse Susan Randal

Matron Jane Randall

Matron Mary Randall

Prescription Clerk D.W. Trowbridge. Gallia County Historical Society.

Matron Viola Randall

Mariah Reynolds

Sarah Reynolds

Laundress Manerva Richison

Matron Sarah Rider

Matron & Laundress Ann E. Robison

Wardmaster William F. Ridgely

Amanda Robinson

Susan Robinson

Cook & Nurse Mary Ann Scisson

Matron Jane Ross

Clerk James W. Searles

George Shankland

Wardmaster Benjamin
F. Udell. Gallia County
Historical Society.

Susan Shankland

Matron Jane Smith

Martha Smith

Matron Mary Smith

Phoebe Smith

Matron Rose Smith

Matron Catharine Snider

Matron Lucy Squalls

Chaplain Henry S. Stevens, 14th
Connecticut Infantry

Matron Jane Steward

Matron Jane Stewart

Rachel Streibling /Stribling

Laundress Nora/Norah Thomas

Matron Jane Thompson

Matron Margaret M. Turner

Prescription Clerk D.W. Trowbridge

Wardmaster Benjamin F. Udell, 23rd
Ohio Infantry

Matron Sue Vanhorn

Matron Celez Waggoner

Julia Walker

Matron Mary Walters

Matron Rebecca Walters

Matron & Nurse Eliza Watkins

Cook & Nurse Reuben West

Cook & Matron Elizabeth J. White

Matron Jane Wiley

Matron & Laundress Margaret Wiley

Matron Naoma Wiley

Matron Mary Willis

State Guard D. I. N. Wilson

Matron Susan Wright

State Guard D.I.N. Wilson.
Gallia County Historical
Society.

APPENDIX C

Nurses of the U.S. Army General Hospital, Gallipolis, Ohio

Nurse Samuel Allen

Nurse Mary Jane Bailey

Nurse Rachael/Rachel Brooks

Nurse Margret Conrod

Nurse Lucy Cornell

Nurse George Debussey/Debussy, Company A, 2nd West Virginia Cavalry

Nurse May S. Freeman

Nurse Elizabeth Graham

Nurse Hellen Hayward/Howard

Nurse Charles Hedrick/Hendrick

Nurse & Matron Susan Lewis

Nurse Jennie Loomis

Nurse Hannah U. Maxon, Medical Department, U.S. Volunteers

Nurse Eliza J. Mulvane, Medical Department, U.S. Volunteers

Nurse & Matron Margaret Randal

Nurse & Matron Mary Randal

Nurse & Matron Susan Randal

Nurse and Matron Ada H. Reynolds, 11th Ohio Infantry

Nurse Susanna Robinson

Nurse Clara Scisson

Nurse Mary Ann Scisson

Nurse Mary Jane Seems

Nurse Altha/Althea Snydam

Nurse John W. Stanton

Nurse Eliza Stone

Nurse Ellen Udell

Nurse Margret Walter

Nurse and Matron Eliza/Elizah Watkins

Nurse Reuben West

Nuns of the Sisters of Charity of Mount St. Vincent, based in Cincinnati, also served as nurses at the hospital: Sister Ambrosia, Sister Basilia, Sister Constantina, Sister Euphrasia, Sister Gonzaga, Sister Laurence, Sister Louis, and Sister Seraphine.

APPENDIX D

Union Soldiers Associated with the USAGH Gallipolis, Ohio

A variety of primary and secondary sources were used to compile this list. Primary sources included correspondence and orders from the hospital, 1864-65, found at the National Library of Medicine Historical Medical Collection at the National Institutes of Health, and correspondence to Surgeon Lincoln R. Stone, documents from the National Archives. Online books also provided important information about soldiers, including Civil War state Adjutant General's records from Ohio and West Virginia, and the *Surgical and Medical History of the War of the Rebellion*. 35th Star author Terry Lowry's book, *The Battle of Charleston*, was a helpful resource. In addition, soldier identifications and proof of their treatment at Gallipolis came from cemetery records, soldiers' letters and diaries, and newspaper articles, among other secondary sources. Gallipolis hospital connections were also verified via fold3.com, familysearch.org and ancestry.com.

There were quite a few challenges involved in confirming the hundreds of men who were at one time or another at the hospital. Many, if not most, were patients in wards. Others, however, were simply examined for discharge or furlough at Gallipolis.

It would be impossible to identify all of the soldiers, either Union or Confederate, who spent time at the U.S. Army Hospital at Gallipolis, so this list is by no means comprehensive. Finding these patients is, at times, a real needle-in-the-haystack process, involving a combination of research, tenacity, and luck. In any event, it is reasonable to assume that a 500-bed hospital that operated from June 1862 until the close of the war accommodated at least close to a thousand soldiers.

Private Frank Abbey, Company A, 47th Ohio Infantry & 13th Ohio Cavalry

Private John Adams, Company H, 34th Ohio Infantry

Private Nelson Adams, Company F, 92nd Ohio Infantry

Private Austin/Austain Adkins, Company B, 8th Virginia (West Virginia Infantry) & 7th West Virginia Cavalry

Private David Adkins, Company G, 8th Virginia (West Virginia) Infantry & 7th West Virginia Cavalry

Private Isom Adkins, 8th Virginia (West Virginia) Infantry & Company L, 7th West Virginia Cavalry

Private Pleasant A. Adkins, Company K, 5th West Virginia Infantry

Corporal James M. Aikin/Aikins, Companies E & K, 47th Ohio Infantry

Private Erastus Aldridge, Company B, 23rd Ohio Infantry

Private George W. Allen, Company B, 23rd Ohio Infantry

Private James Allen, Company D, 14th Virginia (West Virginia) Infantry

Private Lewis D. Allen, Company I, 2nd West Virginia Cavalry

Private David Alexander, Company F, 174th Ohio Infantry

Sergeant Samuel C. Alexander, Company B, 4th West Virginia Infantry

Private Mandiville/Mandaville/Mandival Alstead, Company L, 7th West Virginia Cavalry

Private James M. Anderson, Company H, 4th West Virginia Infantry

Private Benjamin A. Armstrong, Company E, 8th Virginia (West Virginia) Infantry & 7th West Virginia Cavalry

Private Robert Armstrong, Companies A & M, 1st New York Cavalry

Private William Atkins, Company L, 8th Virginia (West Virginia) Infantry & 7th West Virginia Cavalry

Private John Atkinson, Company A, 60th Ohio Infantry

Private John Atkinson/Atkison/Atkisson, Company E, 13th West Virginia Infantry & Company 66, 2nd Battalion Veteran Reserve Corps (organized at Gallipolis, OH, 1863)

Private Newton B. Ayers, Company B, 34th Ohio Infantry

Private Bernhart/Barnhart Baasch/Baash/Bash, Company A, 108th Ohio Infantry

Private Franklin E. Backus, Company G, 4th West Virginia Infantry

Private William Bacmeister/Backmaster, 1st Independent Battery Ohio Light Artillery

Private George W. Baggs, Company B, 36th Ohio Veteran Infantry

Private Lewis Bailes, Company C, 44th Ohio Infantry

Private Edward Baisden, Company F, 5th West Virginia Infantry

Private (First name Unknown) Baker, Company K, 34th Ohio Infantry

Private Reason/Rezin Baker, Company H, 116th Ohio Infantry

Private Solomon Baker, Company B, 21st Ohio Infantry

Quartermaster Sergeant David Baldwin, Company E, 8th Virginia (West Virginia) Infantry & 7th West Virginia Cavalry

Private James B. Ballard, Company I, 8th Virginia (West Virginia) Infantry

Corporal Addison M. Ballenger, & Company D, 8th Virginia (West Virginia) Infantry & 7th West Virginia Cavalry

Private James Ballanger/Ballenger, Company F, 2nd West Virginia Cavalry

Private Clark Barber, Company D, 7th Ohio Infantry

Private Elisha Barber/Barbour, Company A, 5th West Virginia Infantry

Private Francis A. Barnes, Company C, 2nd West Virginia Cavalry

Private George Barnet, Company D, 91st Ohio Infantry

Corporal Aaron/Aram E. Barnett, Company F, 9th Virginia (West Virginia) Infantry

Private Sylvanus Barney, Company I, 4th West Virginia Infantry & Company A, 2nd West Virginia Veteran Infantry

Private Lemon Barr, Company K, 2nd West Virginia Cavalry

Private Titus Barr, Company L, 14th Pennsylvania Cavalry

Private John Barrett, Company E, 44th Ohio Infantry & 8th Ohio Cavalry

Private Calvin Bartlett, Company F 2nd West Virginia Cavalry

Private Robert M. Bartlett, Company I, 16th Ohio Infantry

Saddler Isaac K. Bartley, Company K, 2nd West Virginia Cavalry

Private James L. Barton, Company K, 7th Ohio Cavalry

Regimental Hospital Steward Thomas H. Barton, Company E, 4th West Virginia Infantry

Private Adam Bates, Company G, 73rd Ohio Infantry

Private Spencer Batey, Company B, 116th Ohio Infantry

Regimental Hospital Steward Thomas H. Barton, Co. E, 4th West Virginia Infantry. From *Autobiography of Dr. Thomas H. Barton, the Self-Made Physician of Syracuse, Ohio.*

Private James M. Bayes, & Company K, 8th Virginia (West Virginia) Infantry & 7th West Virginia Cavalry

Private Charles W. Beans, Companies H & I, 98th Ohio Infantry

Private John Beljer/Belger, Company G, 34th Ohio Infantry & Compaony, K, 36th Ohio Infantry

Private Herrick Benjamin, Company K, 26th Ohio Infantry

Private John Benner, Company B, 91st Ohio Infantry

Private Jesse Bennett, 1st Independent Battery, Ohio Light Artillery & Company 66, 2nd Battalion Veteran Reserve Corps (organized at Gallipolis, OH, 1863)

Private Samuel Berger, Company A, 37th Ohio Infantry

Private Jesse Berks, Company G, 13th West Virginia Infantry

Private Josiah Betts, Company H, 123rd Ohio Infantry

Private Granville Beverlin, Company B, 11th West Virginia Infantry

Private Samuel G. Birch, Company G, 26th Ohio Infantry

Private Harvey Bishop, Company F, 7th West Virginia Cavalry

Private William Bishop, Company A, 91st Ohio Infantry

Corporal Augustine Boice, Co. B, 91st Ohio Infantry. Courtesy of Gallia County Genealogical Society.

Private Anton Bissegger, Company D, 37th Ohio Infantry

Private John Blackburn, Company D, 172nd Infantry Ohio National Guard

Private John F. Blackburn, Company D, 13th West Virginia Infantry

Private Andrew J. Blakeman, Company F, 91st Ohio Infantry

Private Ezekiel Blankenship/Blankinship, Company B, 2nd West Virginia Cavalry

Private Joel S. Blankinship, Company B, 91st Ohio Infantry & Company 66, 2nd Battalion Veteran Reserve Corps (organized at Gallipolis, OH, 1863)

Private John P. Blessing, Company F, 34th Ohio Infantry

Private George Bodkin/Bodkins/Botkin/Botkins, Companies I & C, 34th Ohio Infantry

Corporal Augustine Boice, Company B, 91st Ohio Infantry

Private William Bona/Bond, Company A, 16th Ohio Infantry

Private William S. Bonnell, Company H, 21st Ohio Infantry

Private William Booker, Company H, 2nd West Virginia Cavalry

Private John Booton/Booten, Company C, 91st Ohio Infantry

Private Valentine Boovery/Bovery, Simmonds' Battery, Kentucky Light Artillery

Private Daniel C. Bowlen, Company E, West Virginia 7th Cavalry

Private Henry Boyd, Company C, 2nd West Virginia Cavalry

Private Vincent Bradbury, Company B, 34th Ohio Infantry & Company 66, 2nd Battalion Veteran Reserve Corps (organized at Gallipolis, OH, 1863)

1st Lt. Ethan A. Brown, Co. C, 34th Ohio Infantry. Mortally wounded in the head at the Battle of Fayetteville. Died at Gallipolis. Image courtesy of Terry Lowry.

Private Edwin Bradford, Company C, 129th Ohio Infantry and Company I, 44th Ohio Infantry & 8th Ohio Cavalry

Private George Brannon, Company G, 4th Virginia (West Virginia) Infantry

Private Daniel Brandt/Brant, Company B, 8th Ohio Cavalry

Private Frederich Bremer, Company B, 37th Ohio Infantry

Private Adam Brenkman, Company F, 44th Ohio Infantry & 8th Ohio Cavalry

Private Jackson Bridgeford, Company A, 26th Ohio Infantry

Private Adam C. Bridgeman/Bridgman, Companies E & F, 98th Ohio Infantry and Company K, 74th Ohio Infantry

PrivateJames W. Broderick, Company C, 44th Ohio Infantry & 8th Ohio Cavalry

Private Patrick Broderick, Companies I & C, 28th Ohio Infantry

Private Henry Brooks, Company L, 2nd West Virginia Cavalry

Private Josiah T. Brooks, Company F, 4th West Virginia Infantry

Private William Brooks, Company H, 2nd West Virginia Cavalry

Private George Broughton, Company B, 47th Ohio Infantry

Captain Andrew J. Brown, Company B, 12th Ohio Infantry & Company 66, 2nd Battalion Veteran Reserve Corps (organized at Gallipolis, OH, 1863)

Private Charles C. Brown, Company I, 184th Ohio Infantry

1st Lieutenant Ethan A. Brown, Company C, 34th Ohio Infantry

Private Henry Brown, Company C, 11th Ohio Infantry

Corporal John Brown, Company G, 42nd Ohio Infantry

Private John Brown, Company K, 91st Ohio Infantry

Private John Brown, Simmonds' Battery, Kentucky Light Artillery

Private George Brumfield, Company A, 126th Ohio Infantry

Private Joseph Brust, Independent Company, 3rd Ohio Cavalry

Private Washington Bryan/Bryant, Company D, 116th Ohio Infantry

Private Leonard C. Bucey, Company A, 98th Ohio Infantry

Private Charles Bullock, Company C, 103rd Ohio Infantry

Corporal Charles Bundy, Company C, 42nd Ohio Infantry

Private George Bupp, Company H, 26th Ohio Infantry

Private James W. Burage, Company A, 91st Ohio Infantry

Private Eli Burditt, Company A, 2nd West Virginia Veteran Infantry,

Private John A. Burns, Companies C & F, 2nd West Virginia Cavalry

Corporal Nelson N.W.V. Burns, Companies K & E, 47th Ohio Infantry

Private William H. Burnsides, Company H, 2nd West Virginia Cavalry

Private David Burr, Company B, 90th Ohio Infantry

Private William F. Burrows, Company A, 121st Ohio Infantry

Private Joseph Bush, Company I, 34th Ohio Infantry

Private Milo Bushnell, Company D, Trumbull Guards Independent Company, Ohio Infantry

Private William B. Butts, Companies D, F & L, 47th Ohio Infantry

Private Joseph A. Byrnside, Company H, 7th West Virginia Cavalry

Private Hugh W. Caldwell, Company D, 9th Virginia (West Virginia) Infantry

Private David Campbell, Company G, 13th West Virginia Infantry

Private Edward Campbell, Company K, 140th Infantry Ohio National Guard

Private J.W. Campbell, Company I, 14th Pennsylvania Infantry

Corporal Robert Campbell, Company H, 91st Infantry & Company 66, 2nd Battalion Veteran Reserve Corps (organized at Gallipolis, OH, 1863)

Private Abraham Carrahofe/Carrahof, Company F, 23rd Ohio Infantry

Corporal James T./Joseph T. Carey, Company E, 44th Ohio Infantry & 8th Ohio Cavalry

Private John Carmichal/Carmichael, Companies B & G, 2nd West Virginia Cavalry

Private Matthew/Nathan Carpenter, Company C, 9th Virginia (West Virginia) Infantry,

Private Cassius M. Carr, Company A, 172nd Infantry Ohio National Guard

Private John Carson, Company E, 13th West Virginia Infantry

Private Thomas Carson, Company E, 8th Virginia (West Virginia) Infantry & 7th West Virginia Cavalry

Private James Carter, Company H, 1st West Virginia Cavalry

Private John W. Carter, Company K, 3rd West Virginia Cavalry

Private John W. Casa, Company I, 13th West Virginia Infantry

Private James A. Carter, Company H, 1st West Virginia Cavalry

Private Christian Casper, Simmonds' Battery, Kentucky Light Artillery

Private Lester Casterline, Trumbull Guards Independent Company, Ohio Infantry

Private James L. Chapman, Company H, 42nd Ohio Infantry

Private William Chapman, Company E, 22nd Kentucky Infantry

Sergeant George W. Chappell, Company E, 5th West Virginia Infantry & Company 66, 2nd Battalion Veteran Reserve Corps (organized at Gallipolis, OH, 1863)

Private Robert Chappel/Chappell/Chapple, Simmonds' Battery, Kentucky Light Artillery

Private James P. Chase, Company E, 4th West Virginia Infantry

Private Samuel R. Chase, Company B, 37th Iowa Infantry

Private William Chase, Company F, 4th Michigan Cavalry

Private Robert S. Chenney/Chenny, Company L, 7th Ohio Cavalry

Bugler David W. Cherrington, Company H, 2nd Cavalry, Virginia (West Virginia)

Private George W. Christian, Company I, 13th West Virginia Infantry

Private Isaac Christian, Company A, 5th West Virginia Infantry

Private Isaac Clark, Companies B & H, 47th Ohio Infantry

Private Jacob Clark, Company D, 116th Ohio Infantry

Private William H. Clark, Company M, 7th Ohio Cavalry

Private Thomas J. Clegg, Company E, 116th Ohio Infantry

Private Francis M. Clemmings, Company C, 73rd Ohio Infantry

Private Isaac W. Clinger, Company I, 26th Ohio Infantry

Private Edward S. Clithers, Company D, 116th Ohio Infantry

Private Alexander Clonch, Company C, 13th West Virginia Infantry

Private John M. Coalman/Coleman, Company I, 34th Ohio Infantry & Company C, 36th Ohio Infantry

Corporal Abraham Cochran, Company K, 2nd West Virginia Cavalry

Wagoner Edwin S. Codner, Companies B & H, 47th Ohio Infantry

Private Charles G.W. Cole, Company D 34th Ohio Infantry & Company M, 1st Ohio Heavy Artillery

Private Samuel N. Coleman, Company A, 8th Virginia (West Virginia) Infantry & 7th West Virginia Cavalry

Private Isaac T. Collier, Company D, 44th Ohio Infantry & 8th Ohio Cavalry; Company F, 154th Ohio; Company E, 12th Ohio Infantry and Company K, 186th Ohio Infantry

Private Alexander Clonch and wife, Co. C, 13th West Virginia Infantry. Courtesy of Cathy Meder Dempsey.

Sergeant George B. Collins, Company E, 44th Ohio Infantry & 8th Ohio Cavalry

Private Isaac Collins, Company F, 5th West Virginia Infantry

Sergeant Lewis M. Collins, Company A, 5th Tennessee Infantry

Private William A. Colter/Coulter, Company D, 7th Ohio Infantry

Private Joseph P. Coombs, Company A, 34th Ohio Infantry

Private Michael Coney, Company B, 47th Ohio Infantry

Private Harvey F. Conklin, Company G, 11th Ohio Infantry

Private William Conley/Connely, Company A, 22nd Kentucky Infantry

Private Vincent Conner/Connor, Company F, 34th & 36th Ohio Infantry and 7th Veteran Reserve Corps

Private Alonzo Conoway, Company K, 34th Ohio Infantry

Private Fletcher B. Conrad, Company B, 11th West Virginia Infantry

Private Andrew J. Conway, Company G, 34th Ohio Veteran Infantry

Private Henry F. Cook, Company G, 8th Virginia (West Virginia) Infantry,

Private Austin Cooper, Company I, 8th Virginia (West Virginia) Infantry & 7th West Virginia Cavalry

Private Christopher Cooper, Company B, 116th Ohio Infantry

Private Richard M. Corbin, Company K, 44th Ohio Infantry & 8th Ohio Cavalry

Private Jordon Corn, Company D, 91st Ohio Infantry

Private George W. Cornell, Company B, 173rd Ohio Infantry

Private Wesley V. Cosper, Company H, 88th Indiana Infantry

Private William J. Covanovan, Company D, 11th West Virginia Infantry

Private Samuel Coverston, Trumbull Guards Independent Company, Ohio Infantry

Private Enoch W. Cox, Company E, 7th West Virginia Cavalry

Regimental Hospital Steward and Veterinary Surgeon Francis M. Cox, Company A & Field and Staff, 8th Virginia (West Virginia) Infantry & 7th West Virginia Cavalry

Private Josiah Cox, Company K, 21st Ohio Infantry

Private John Craig, Company I, 4th Virginia (West Virginia) Infantry,

Corporal Peter H. Craig, Company G, 2nd West Virginia Cavalry

Private Thomas Craig, Company B, 37th Iowa Infantry

Private James Crane, Company F, 7th West Virginia Cavalry

Private George H. Crawford, Company D, 91st Ohio Infantry

Private William H. Cremeans/Cremeens, Company I, 13th West Virginia Infantry

Private Worthy S. Crippin, Companies D & E, 174th Ohio Infantry

Private William Cripps, Company L, 7th Ohio Cavalry

Private James Croghan, Company B, 37th Iowa Infantry

Private Robert Cromer, Company A, 44th Ohio Infantry & 8th Ohio Cavalry

Private Gilbert Crouch, Company G, 4th West Virginia Infantry

Private David Crumrine/Crumrin, Company B, 44th Ohio Infantry & 8th Ohio Cavalry

Lieutenant G.W. Cuiles, United States Colored Troops** This name is probably a transcription mistake. A George W. Cowles, Company G, 41st United States Colored Troops was recorded on a Returns card as being sick in a General Hospital in March 1865, location not given. On March 20, 1865, Surgeon Lincoln R. Stone wrote a letter to the Medical Director, U.S. Volunteers, stating he had examined Lt. G.W. Cuiles, who had been shot in the left eye and was unable to travel and unfit to return to duty for almost another month. This is an educated guess that Cuiles and Cowles could be the same person, although Cowles was listed on Returns as a Private.

Private Thomas Cumming/Cummings, Company H, 53rd Ohio Infantry

Musician Francis Cumpson/Cumpston, Company C, 9th West Virginia Infantry

Private David Cunningham, Company I, 15th West Virginia Infantry

Private John Cunningham, Company B, 37th Iowa Infantry

Private Vincent Dailey, Company D, 91st Ohio Infantry

Private John Daniels, Company B, 2nd West Virginia Cavalry

Private Aaron B. Dansberry, Independent Company, 1st Battery Ohio Light Artillery

Private Sylvanus Darst, Company K, 26th Ohio Infantry

Private Thomas W. Davis, Company I, 13th West Virginia Infantry

Private Pembroke Davison, Company B, 34th Ohio Infantry

Private Thomas A. Daywalt, Company A, 91st Ohio Infantry

Private Isaac Dean, Company H, 21st Michigan Infantry

Private Thomas Dean, Company A, 4th West Virginia Infantry & 2nd West Virginia Veteran Infantry

Hospital Steward George Debussey/Debussy, Company A and F&S, 2nd West Virginia Cavalry

Private William Deffendoffer, Diffendoffer, Company K, 44th Ohio Infantry & 8th Ohio Cavalry

Private Conrad Deitz/Dietz, Company L, 4th Kentucky Veteran Cavalry

Private James Deming, Company B, 37th Iowa Infantry

Private Harvey Denney, Company L, 7th Ohio Cavalry

Private James Denny, Company C, 13th West Virginia Infantry

Private Edward S. Devine, Company D, 12th Ohio Infantry

Private Samuel Devol, Company F, 2nd West Virginia Cavalry

Private John Dickey, Company I, 91st Ohio Infantry

Private John Dietres/Ditres, Compaony C, 37th Ohio Infantry

Private Isaac Dingey, Company D, 13th West Virginia Infantry

Private Henry Dixon, Company D, 2nd West Virginia Cavalry

Private Alfred Dodson, Company D, 91st Ohio Infantry

Private George W. Doggett, Company K, 191st Ohio Infantry

Private Sylvester Donley, Company K, 21st Ohio Infantry

Private John Donivan/Donnivan, Company A, 2nd Kentucky Infantry

Private Alfred Donovan, Company I, 34th Ohio Infantry

Private Lorenzo Dormon/Dornon, Company K, 2nd Ohio Cavalry

Private James Dorsey, Company H, 9th West Virginia Infantry

Private James B. Douglass, Company G, 8th Virginia (West Virginia) Infantry & 7th West Virginia Cavalry

Corporal Hiram Douglass, Company B, 8th Virginia (West Virginia) Infantry & 7th West Virginia Cavalry

Private James E. Douglass, Company B, 8th Virginia (West Virginia) Infantry & 7th West Virginia Cavalry

Private Wyatt Dowdy, Company A, 91st Ohio Infantry

Private William Downs, Company G, 4th West Virginia Infantry

Private Osborn T. Drake, Company I, 9th West Virginia Infantry

Private Frederick Drew, Company B, 37th Iowa Infantry

Private James Driver, Company A, 4th West Virginia Infantry

Private John Dugan, Company B, 121st Ohio Infantry

Private Wiley Lewis Dugger, Company K, 1st Tennessee Infantry

Corporal William M. Dungan, Companies E & K, 47th Ohio Infantry

Private Frank Dunham, Company B, 34th Ohio Infantry

Private John Dunham, Company B, 34th Ohio Infantry

Private James Dupler, Company A, 92nd Ohio Infantry

Private Ampuda Earwood/Erewood, Company L, 7th Ohio Cavalry

Private Andrew Eby, Company D, 2nd West Virginia Cavalry

Private William R. Eckard, Company B, 13th West Virginia Infantry

Private Martin V.B. Edens, Company A, 13th West Virginia Infantry

Corporal Charles Edleman, Company H, 91st Ohio Infantry

Private David H. Edwards, Company B, 91st Ohio Infantry

Private Harrison Edwards, Company F, 13th West Virginia Infantry

Private Herrman/Heinrich Effing, Companies K & I, 28th Ohio Infantry

Private John Ehlen, Company C, 37th Ohio Infantry, Ohio

Commissary Sergeant Richard Elkins, Company I, 8th Virginia (West Virginia) Infantry & 7th West Virginia Cavalry

Private Chaplin Elliott, Unassigned Company 184th Ohio Infantry & Company C, 191st Ohio Infantry

Private Daniel M. Elliott, Company I, 14th Illinois Cavalry

Private James H. Elliott, Company G, 172nd Infantry Ohio National Guard

Private Cornelius H. Ellis, Company D, 5th West Virginia Infantry & Company E, 1st West Virginia Veteran Infantry

Private Lawrence Elsaesser, Company D, 37th Ohio Infantry

Private Philip/Phillipp Emery, Company G, 91st Ohio Infantry & Company 66, 2nd Battalion Veteran Reserve Corps (organized at Gallipolis, OH, 1863)

Private Lewis/Louis Emmert, Company H, 91st Ohio Infantry

Private Peola Eno, Company B, 91st Ohio Infantry

Private Albert L. Entrican, Company K, 21st Michigan Infantry

Private DeWitt C. Eskings, Company H, 8th Virginia (West Virginia) Mounted Infantry & 7th West Virginia Cavalry

Private Michael Esselon, Company C, 5th New York Heavy Artillery

Corporal Isaac N. Evans, Company C, 44th Ohio Infantry & 8th Ohio Cavalry

Private Mitchell Evans, Company B, 8th Virginia (West Virginia) Infantry & 7th West Virginia Cavalry

Lieutenant Henry Everman, Company H, 22nd Kentucky Infantry

1st Lieutenant Elmore E. Ewing, Companies A & K, 91st Ohio Infantry

Private Vincent C. Ewing, Companies A & E, 34th Ohio Infantry

Private William Ewing, Company K, 91st Ohio Infantry

Private Alexander A. Fackler, Company K, 98th Ohio Infantry

Private William A. Fall, Company I, 2nd West Virginia Cavalry

Private George Fankell, Company A, McLaughlin's Squadron Ohio Volunteer Cavalry

Private Harvey H. Farley, Company D, 5th West Virginia Infantry

Private John Fausnet, Company D, 5th West Virginia Infantry

Private William H. Fauver, Company C, 8th Virginia (West Virginia) Infantry & 7th West Virginia Cavalry

Private Alverd/Olverd B. Fay, Company H, 44th Ohio Infantry & 8th Ohio Cavalry and Company K, 113th Ohio Infantry

Private John Feirbaugh/Firebaugh/Freibaugh, Company G, 1st Ohio Heavy Artillery

Private Louis Gotlieb Fenster, Company G, 91st Ohio Infantry

Private Benjamin F. Ferguson/Furgeson, Company F, 44th Ohio Infantry & 8th Ohio Cavalry

Private John H. Ferguson/Furgison, Company D, 91st Ohio Infantry

Private Malcolm S. Ferguson, Trumbull Guards Independent Company, Ohio Infantry

Sergeant William I. Fickey, Company K, 26th Ohio Infantry

Private Eli Fipps, Company H, 8th Virginia (West Virginia) Infantry & 7th West Virginia Cavalry

Private Joseph A./H. Fisher, Company F, 44th Ohio Infantry & 8th Ohio Cavalry

Private John Fitzpatrick, Company F, 2nd West Virginia Cavalry

Private William Flack, Company K, 91st Ohio Infantry

Private Samuel V. Flack/Fleck/Flake, Companies A & H, 13th West Virginia Infantry

Private John Fletcher, Companies B & K, 121st Ohio Infantry

Private James A. Flora/Floary, Company M, 7th Ohio Cavalry

Private George W. Flowers, Company I, 9th West Virginia Infantry

Private James J. Forbush, Company I, 13th West Virginia Infantry & Company G, 4th West Virginia Infantry

Private Adam C. Forney, Companies E & K, 23rd Ohio Infantry

Private Thomas B. Fouty, Company C, 2nd West Virginia Cavalry

Corporal Richard Fowler, Company A, 11th West Virginia Infantry

Private Sylvester Foy, Company C, 34th Ohio Infantry

Private Jeremiah "Jerry" D. Freer, Trumbull Guards Independent Company, Ohio Infantry

Chaplain Russell G. French, F & S, 23rd Ohio Infantry

Private William Freshour, Company E, 8th Ohio Infantry

Private Theodore/Theodule/Theochile Froideveaux, Company G, 92nd Ohio Infantry

Private Henry J. Fry, Company G, 4th West Virginia Infantry

Private George V. Fullen/Fuller, Company C, 5th West Virginia Infantry

Private Charles E. Fuller, Company F, 91st Ohio Infantry

Private Winfield S. Fulton, Company F, 98th Ohio Infantry

Private Jacob Funk, Company D, 36th Ohio Infantry

Private Jesse Gannon, Company D, 126th Ohio Infantry

Private William Gard, Company B, 37th Iowa Infantry

Private Joseph Gardner, Company C, 193rd Ohio Infantry

Private John E. Garrison, Companies K & E, 47th Ohio Infantry

Private William W. Garrison, Company E, 47th Ohio Infantry

Private William Garnett, Company E, 11th Ohio Infantry

Private Stephen P. Gates, Company B, 2nd West Virginia Cavalry

Private August Geist, Company A, 37th Ohio Infantry

Private James E. Gibson, Company L, 7th West Virginia Veteran Cavalry

Private Miles T. Gibson, Independent Company, Trumbull Guards, Ohio

Private Hamilton Giles, Company B, 12th West Virginia Infantry

Private Ira H. Gilkey, Company A, 2nd West Virginia Cavalry

Private William Gill, Company G, 3rd Ohio Cavalry & Company 66, 2nd Battalion Veteran Reserve Corps (organized at Gallipolis, OH, 1863)

Private Jacob Gillin/Gilland/Gililand, Company F, 27th Ohio Infantry & Company I, 140th Infantry Ohio National Guard

Private John Gillespie/Gillispie, Company I, 60th Ohio Infantry

Private Rowland Gillespie, Company F, 8th Virginia (West Virginia) Infantry & 7th West Virginia Cavalry

Sergeant James Gills, Company B, 91st Ohio Infantry

Private Charles W. Gist, Company E, 122nd Ohio Infantry

Private Peter Goddard, Company H, 2nd West Virginia Cavalry

Corporal Asa Goodrich, Company B, 23rd Ohio Infantry & Company 66, 2nd Battalion Veteran Reserve Corps (organized at Gallipolis, OH, 1863)

Private Israel Gooseman, Company C, 2nd West Virginia Cavalry & Company H, 7th Battalion Veteran Reserve Corps

Private John Gorby, Company K, 15th West Virginia Infantry

Private James M. Gorell/Gorsell, Company E, 111th Ohio Infantry

Private Ralph H. Gorham, Companies D & I, 2nd Ohio Cavalry

Private John Gorman, Company C, 13th West Virginia Infantry

Private Joseph Gossett, Company E, 5th West Virginia Infantry

Private Daniel W. Gould, Company B, 97th Ohio Infantry

Private Sidney J. Graham, Company H, 21st Ohio Infantry

Musician Emerson R. Grant, Company G, 195th Ohio Infantry, Unassigned Company, 186th Ohio Infantry & Company H, 140th Ohio National Guard

Private George W. Grant, Company D, 1st Kentucky Infantry

Private James E. Grant, Simmonds' Battery, Kentucky Light Artillery

Private Michael Gratz, Company A, 28th Ohio Infantry

Private William H. Greathouse, Company H, 13th West Virginia Infantry

Private John Green/Greene, Company B, 37th Iowa Infantry

Private Theodore Greenwood, Company I, 44th Ohio Infantry & 8th Ohio Cavalry

Private Isaiah Griffin, Company E, 9th West Virginia Infantry

Private Morris Griffith, Company I, 12th Ohio Infantry & Company 66, 2nd Battalion Veteran Reserve Corps (organized at Gallipolis, OH, 1863)

Private Alexander A. Grossman, Company H, 2nd West Virginia Cavalry

Private Alloyse Gullet, Company C, 28th Ohio Infantry

Private John Gunther, Company B, 26th Ohio Infantry

Corporal Silas Hager/Hagar, Company G, 7th West Virginia Cavalry

Private Jacob Hagerman/Hagaman, Company I, 34th Ohio Infantry

Private Orange Haize, Company K, 121st Ohio Infantry

Private Daniel M. Hall, Companies E & K, 47th Ohio Infantry

Lieutenant Colonel James R. Hall, Field & Staff, 13th West Virginia Infantry

Private Martin Hall, Company C, 5th West Virginia Infantry

Private Robert Hall, Company F, 30th Ohio Infantry

Private George Hamilton, Company E, 7th West Virginia Cavalry

Private Isaac Hamilton, Company E, 2nd West Virginia Cavalry

Private Elisha Hammer, Companies E & K, 47th Ohio Infantry

Private Lewis/Louis A. Hammer, Companies E & K, 47th Ohio Infantry & Company F, 88th Ohio Infantry

Private Henry Hammon/Hammond/Hamon, 1st Independent Battery, Ohio Light Artillery

1st Lieutenant James W. Hanna, Field & Staff, 13th West Virginia Infantry

Private Edward Hanrahan/Hannehan, Company C, 34th Ohio Infantry

Private William Hardee, Company D, 9th West Virginia Infantry & 1st West Virginia Veteran Infantry

Private William Harkins, Company K, 9th Ohio Infantry

Private James B. Harless, Company B, 8th Virginia (West Virginia) Infantry & 7th West Virginia Cavalry

Corporal Myron Harper, Company C, 30th Ohio Cavalry

1st Lieutenant William H. Hassinger, Company A, 55th Ohio Infantry

Private Mark E. Hathaway, Company A, 44th Ohio Infantry & 8th Ohio Cavalry

Private Solomon F. Hawk, Companies I & B, 2nd West Virginia Cavalry

1st Lieutenant Peter M. Hawke, Company H, 8th Ohio Infantry

Private Edmund S. Hawkins, Company A, 34th Ohio Infantry

Private Jonathan Hawkins, Company K, 15th West Virginia Infantry

Private David S. Hayes/Hays, Companies I & E, 34th Ohio Infantry

Private James Hayes/Hays, Company B, 13th West Virginia Infantry

Private John Hays, Company F, 13th West Virginia Infantry

1st Sergeant Franklin/Francis Haynes, Company F, 8th Virginia (West Virginia) Infantry & 7th West Virginia Cavalry

Private John Haynes, Company B, 9th West Virginia Infantry & 1st West Virginia Veteran Infantry

Private Jacob Hays, Company G, 60th Ohio Infantry

Private John Hays, Company F, 13th West Virginia Infantry

Private Thomas Hays, Company D, 4th Tennessee Mounted Infantry

Private James R. Hedges, Company I, 34th Ohio Infantry & 38th Ohio Infantry

Private George Held, Company B, 37th Ohio Infantry

Private Nicholas Helfric, Company H, 44th Ohio Infantry & 8th Ohio Cavalry

Private Harry Helm, Company K, 122nd U.S. Colored Troops Infantry

Private Cyrus Henry, Company G, 21st Ohio Militia

Blacksmith James W. Henthorn, Company K, 2nd West Virginia Cavalry

Private Samuel Henthorn, Company E, 116th Ohio Infantry

Private Charles A. Herman, Company F, 44th Ohio Infantry; Company K, 8th Ohio Cavalry; 1st Ohio Heavy Artillery; & Company 245, 1st Battalion Veteran Reserve Corps

Private John Herrold, Company D, 2nd Ohio Cavalry

Private John Hesson, Company E, 36th Ohio Infantry

Private Elias Hickle, Company E, 172nd Infantry Ohio National Guard

Private Jonathan Hickman, Company A, 44th Ohio Infantry & 8th Ohio Cavalry

Private William R. Hickman, Company D, 9th West Virginia Infantry

Private James A. Hill, Company K, 13th West Virginia Infantry

Private Jesse L. Hill, Company K, 13th West Virginia Infantry

Private Jonathan Hill, Company K, 13th West Virginia Infantry

Private Nathan Hill, Company K, 172nd Infantry Ohio National Guard

Private James M. Hobough, Company C, 2nd West Virginia Cavalry

Corporal James H. Hoffman, Company E, 8th Virginia (West Virginia) Infantry & 7th West Virginia Cavalry

Private John Hogue, Company H, 91st Ohio Infantry

2nd Lieutenant Edward M. Hoit, Company D, 14th West Virginia Infantry

Private John T. Holland, Company H, 92nd Ohio Infantry

Private William T. Holmes, Company I, 8th Virginia (West Virginia) Infantry & 7th West Virginia Cavalry

Private William Honeywell, Company B, 21st Ohio Infantry

Private Charles Hooper, Company C, 34th Massachusetts Infantry

Private James H. Hopkins, Company C, 88th Ohio Infantry

Quartermaster Sergeant Marcus S. Hopkins, Companies F, E & K, 7th Ohio Infantry & Company D, 9th Battalion Veteran Reserve Corps

Private Uriah Horney, Company D, 44th Ohio Infantry & 8th Ohio Cavalry

Private Antony Hornung, Companies I & K, 47th Ohio Infantry

Corporal Simrell Hoskins/Huskins, Company E, 3rd Tennessee Infantry

Private Davis J. Howard, Company E, 121st Ohio Infantry

Farrier George W. Hughes, Company K, 8th Virginia (West Virginia) Infantry & 7th West Virginia Cavalry

Private Franklin D. Hunt, Independent Company, 3rd Ohio Cavalry

Private Andrew S. Hunter, Company G, 60th Ohio Infantry

Private Henry C. Hunter, Company K, 13th West Virginia Infantry

Private Peter Hurley, Company B, 44th Ohio Infantry & 8th Ohio Cavalry

Private Samuel P. Hysell, Company A, 2nd West Virginia Cavalry

Private William F. Irwin/Irvin/Ervin, Company A, 34th Ohio Infantry

Private William Jackson, Company D, 13th West Virginia, Infantry

Corporal David G. Jacobs, Company I, 8th Ohio Cavalry

Private Nathaniel James, Company F, 2nd Ohio Heavy Artillery

Sergeant George F. Jarrell, Company B, 5th West Virginia Infantry & Company F, 1st West Virginia Veteran Infantry

Private Felix Jeffries, Company B, 13th West Virginia Infantry

Private Charles L./S. Jenkins, Company B, 91st Ohio Infantry

Musician Thomas J. Jenkins, Company H, 9th West Virginia Infantry

Private David C. Johnson, Company E, 47th Ohio Infantry

Private Elmer A. Johnson, Company D, 2nd West Virginia Cavalry

Private Henry M. Johnson, Company K, 3rd West Virginia Cavalry

1st Sergeant John W. Johnson, Company C, 1st Ohio Cavalry

Private Robert Johnson, Company C, 5th West Virginia Infantry

Private Andrew J. Jolly, Company H, 13th Ohio Infantry & Company 66, 2nd Battalion Veteran Reserve Corps (organized at Gallipolis, OH, 1863)

Private Andrew Jones, Company B, 5th West Virginia Infantry

Private Asa Jones, Company K, 13th West Virginia Infantry

Private Byron Jones, Company F, 47th Ohio Infantry & Company K, 172nd Infantry Ohio National Guard

Corporal David E.F. Jones, Company H, 2nd West Virginia Cavalry

Private Emanuel Jones, Company D, 2nd West Virginia Cavalry

Private Nathaniel Jones, Company F, 2nd Ohio Heavy Artillery

Private Stephen Jones, Company E, 22nd Kentucky Infantry

Private Clement Joseph, Company E, 47th Ohio Infantry

Private Nathan B. Joseph, Company E, 47th Ohio Infantry

Private Israel Justice, Company C, 5th West Virginia Infantry

Private William Justice, Company K, 5th West Virginia Infantry

Private William Keebaugh, Company C, 11th West Virginia Infantry

Private James Kelly, Company L, 2nd West Virginia Cavalry

Private James A. Kelley/Kelly, Company D, 91st Ohio Infantry

Private James W. Kelly, Companies A & G, 1st West Virginia Cavalry & Company 66, 2nd Battalion Veteran Reserve Corps (organized at Gallipolis, OH, 1863)

Private Levi T. Kendig/Kindig, Company F, 16th Ohio Infantry

Sergeant John Kennedy, Company K, 7th Ohio Cavalry

Private William Kennedy, Company A, 44th Ohio Infantry & 8th Ohio Cavalry

Private Edward J. Keplinger, Company I, 44th Ohio Infantry & 8th Ohio Cavalry

Private George W. Kernell, Company B, 91st Ohio Infantry

Corporal Peter L. Kernell, Company B, 91st Ohio Infantry

Private Ausmer King, Company D, 5th West Virginia Infantry

Private Thomas B. King, Company A, 2nd West Virginia Cavalry

Private Thomas R. King, 1st Independent Battery, Ohio Light Artillery & Company 66, 2nd Battalion Veteran Reserve Corps (organized at Gallipolis, OH, 1863)

Private John Kirk, Company D, 9th West Virginia Infantry

Private Adam Kluter, Simmonds' Battery, Kentucky Light Artillery

Private Samuel P. Knapp, Company H, 9th West Virginia Infantry

Private Enoch Kneel/Neal, Company C, 5th West Virginia Infantry

Private Charles Kolb, Company C, 47th Ohio Infantry

Private Adam Kolt, Company H, 44th Ohio Infantry & 8th Ohio Cavalry

Private Henry Kramer, Company G, 12th Ohio Infantry & Company K, 23rd Ohio Infantry

Private John M. Krise, Company E, 44th Ohio Infantry & 8th Ohio Cavalry

Private Louis Krueger/Kruger, Company B, 37th Ohio Infantry

Private Henry Kuttner/Kurtner, Company I, 37th Ohio Infantry

James H. LaFarree, Private, Company C, 21st Ohio Infantry & 1st Sergeant, Company G, 189th Ohio Infantry

Corporal Isaac Latimore, Company B, 75th Ohio Infantry

Private Hiram Laughlin, Company G, 91st Ohio Infantry

Wagoner Patrick Laughlin/Laughrin, Company F, 55th Ohio Infantry

Private John Williams Lawless, Company Unassigned, 23rd Ohio Infantry

Private Dewitt C. Lawson, Company A, 14th Pennsylvania Cavalry

Private John M. Layne, Company A, 9th West Virginia Infantry

Private John W. Leaper, Company B, 91st Ohio Infantry

Private George Ledom/Leedom, Company D, 34th Ohio Infantry

Private Harrison P. Lee, Company H, 18th Ohio Infantry & Company I, 2nd West Virginia Cavalry

1st Lieutenant & Quartermaster James A. Leisure, F & S, 13th Ohio Infantry

Private James Legg, Company E, 13th West Virginia Infantry

Private John Lewis, Company I, 36th Ohio Infantry

Private Gottlieb Lidle, Company I, 37th Ohio Infantry

Private Christian Limbaugh, Simmonds' Battery, 1st Light Artillery, Kentucky

Private Abram Lindley/Lindlay, Company F, 11th Ohio Infantry

Private Franz Lippart, Company A, 28th Ohio Infantry

Private Joseph M. Lippincott, Company B, 50th Ohio Infantry

Private John Lober, Company I, 37th Ohio Infantry

Private John Lomax, Company F, 30th Ohio Infantry

Private William Longbrake, Company F, 44th Ohio Infantry & 8th Ohio Cavalry

Private Hart E. Loomis, Company B, 23rd Ohio Infantry

Private John Lorie, Loarie, Company C, 2nd West Virginia Cavalry

Private Abraham Loudon, Company C, 59th Ohio Infantry

Private Arthur Love, Company A, 2nd West Virginia Cavalry

Private Friedrich/Frederick Loving/Leiving/Lewing, Company B, 34th Ohio Infantry

Corporal Charles Low, Company B, 47th Ohio Infantry

Private Martin B. Loy, Company D, 44th Ohio Infantry & 8th Ohio Cavalry

Private Andrew Lucas, Company F, 172nd Infantry Ohio National Guard

Private Nathan Lukingbeal/Lukingbill, Company K, 2nd Ohio Cavalry

Private James E. Lunsford, Company I, 13th West Virginia Infantry

Private David H. Luther, Company B, 5th West Virginia Infantry

Private George B. Lynch, Company C, 2nd West Virginia Cavalry

Private Joseph Lyons, Company C, 9th West Virginia Infantry

Corporal John Magoon, Company K, 91st Ohio Infantry

Private Patrick Mahon, Company D, 14th Pennsylvania Cavalry

Private Joseph Mann, Company H, 121st Ohio Infantry

Private Joel Mannon, Company K, 2nd Ohio Cavalry

Private Edward Mansfield, Company K, 91st Ohio Infantry

Private James Markel, Company G, 2nd West Virginia Cavalry

Private John D. Markel/Markle, Company D, 91st Ohio Infantry

Sergeant Cornelius Markin, Company H, 9th West Virginia Infantry

Private Calvin Marsh, Company H, 130th Infantry Ohio National Guard

Private Finley Marshall, Company H, 91st Ohio Infantry

Private Albert Martin, Company C, 5th West Virginia Infantry

Private Marshall Martin, Company C, 98th Ohio Infantry

Private Thomas Martin, Company D, 5th Ohio Cavalry

Private Moses Massie, Company A, 91st Ohio Infantry

Private Alexander Mathers, Company D, 75th Ohio Infantry

Private Andrew Mayhew/Mayhugh, Company K, 3rd West Virginia Cavalry

Private John W. Mayes/Mays, Company E, 47th Ohio Infantry & Company H, 13th Ohio Cavalry

Private Samuel McCain, Company F, 91st Ohio Infantry

Private William B. McCauley, Company C, 13th West Virginia Infantry

Sergeant John McClintock/McClintic, Company D, 8th Ohio Cavalry

Private Robert M. McClure/McChure, McMullin's Battery, 1st Ohio Light Artillery

Private Daniel McCloud/McLoud, Company C, 13th West Virginia Infantry

Private William McConnaha, Company B, 34th Ohio Infantry

Private Jackson McConnell, Company D, 126th Ohio Infantry

Sergeant James H. McCormick, Company F, 2nd Ohio Heavy Artillery

Private James J.B. McCormick, Company F, 23rd Michigan Infantry

Private Robert E. McCormick, Company F, 34th Ohio Infantry

Private James R. McCoy, Company F, 13th West Virginia Infantry

Private Robert S. McCoy, Company E, 3rd West Virginia Cavalry

Private George McDade, Company E, 7th West Virginia Cavalry

Private John McDaniel, Company B, 13th West Virginia Infantry

Private James McDaniel, Company G, 11th Ohio Infantry

Corporal Stephen B. McDaniel/McDaniels, Company C, 11th Ohio Infantry

Private Thomas McElroy/McIlroy, Company C, 34th Ohio Infantry

Private Green McGee, Company C, 91st Ohio Infantry

Private Charles McGraw, Compaony B, 5th West Virginia Infantry

Private Thomas McGuire, Company K, 91st Ohio Infantry

Private George W. McKee, Company F, 91st Ohio Infantry

Private Samuel M. McKee, Company B, 5th Virginia (West Virginia) Infantry,

Private John McKown, Company K, 9th Virginia (West Virginia) Infantry

Private John L. McMaster, Companies A & E, 2nd West Virginia Cavalry

Private Andrew D. McNealy, Company B, 8th Virginia (West Virginia) Infantry & 7th West Virginia Cavalry

Private Edgar Meehan/Mehan/Mehen, Companies F & C, 34th Ohio Infantry

Private James Melvine, Companies A & C, 47th Ohio Infantry

Private John Menough, Company B, 7th Ohio Cavalry

Corporal Robert Merrill, Company A, 2nd West Virginia Veteran Cavalry

Captain Elija R. Merriman, Company F, 5th West Virginia Infantry

Private Joseph Metcalf/Medcalf, Company F, 2nd West Virginia Infantry

Private Herrmann Meyer, Companies D & G, 28th Ohio Infantry

Private William Michael, Company B, 3rd West Virginia Cavalry

Private James Miers/Myers, Company H, 9th West Virginia Infantry

Private James Milherne/Millhorn/Millhurn, Company K, 2nd West Virginia Cavalry

Corporal Asberry/Asbury J. Miller, Company E, 172nd Infantry Ohio National Guard

Private Charles Miller, Company N, 2nd Kentucky Infantry

Private Norman Miller, Company B, 52nd Ohio Infantry

Corporal James B. Miller, Company G., 116th Ohio Infantry

Private Samuel Miller, Company C, 123rd Ohio Infantry

Private William Miller, Company I, 2nd West Virginia Cavalry

Private William H. Miller, Company A, 37th Iowa Infantry

Wagoner Wilson A. Miller, Company G, 7th West Virginia Cavalry

Corporal Ira Minier, Company B, 37th Iowa Infantry

Private George W. Minks, 8th Independent Company, Ohio Sharp Shooters

Private John J. Mitchell, Company I, 8th Virginia (West Virginia) Infantry & 7th West Virginia Cavalry

Private Lafayette Mitchell, Company D, 21st Ohio Infantry

Private William Mitchell, Companies B & G, 2nd West Virginia Cavalry

Private William Mitchell, Company A, 4th West Virginia Infantry & Company G, 5th West Virginia Infantry

Corporal Arnold Mollohan/Molohan, Company M, 3rd West Virginia Cavalry

Private William Moody, Company G, 34th Ohio Infantry

Private Henry H. Moon, Companies E & K, 47th Ohio Infantry

Private Lewis A. Mooney, Company L, 7th West Virginia Cavalry

Private James Moore, Company H, 118th Ohio Infantry

Private James A. Moore/More, Company M, 7th Ohio Cavalry

Corporal James W. Morgan, Company G, 36th Ohio Infantry

Private Robert E. Morrow, Company B, 4th West Virginia Infantry

Private Peter/P.T. Morton, Company D, 1st Pennsylvania Provisional Cavalry & Company H, 2nd Pennsylvania Cavalry

Private Enos. C. Mulford, Company E, 9th West Virginia Infantry

Private Thomas Mulligan, Company B, 141st Ohio Infantry

Private James H. Murphy, Company H, 13th West Virginia Infantry

Private William Murray/Murry, Company A, 2nd West Virginia Cavalry

Private Wilber/Wilbur/William Myers, Company E, 44th Ohio Infantry

Private George Nance, Company H, 9th West Virginia Infantry

Private Frederick Napoleon, Companies I & C, 28th Ohio Infantry

Private Simeon Neal, Company C, 5th West Virginia Infantry

Sergeant Lewis S. Nease, Company A, 2nd West Virginia Cavalry

Private Samuel W. Nester, Company C, 11th West Virginia Infantry. Image courtesy descendant Richard Nester.

Private Alvis Neiderraggar/Neidereggar, Company F, 34th Ohio Infantry

Private William R. Nessel, Companies B & H, 47th Ohio Infantry

Private Samuel W. Nester, Company C, 11th West Virginia Infantry

2nd Lieutenant Thomas Newcomb, Company F, 8th Virginia (West Virginia) Infantry & 7th West Virginia Cavalry

Private Benjamin R. Newman, Company D, 34th Ohio Infantry

Private Zachariah Nicely, Company D, 9th West Virginia Infantry & Company B, 1st West Virginia Veteran Infantry

Private William T. Nichols, Company G, 4th West Virginia Infantry

Private Samuel Nieberger, Company I, 44th Ohio Infantry & 8th Ohio Cavalry

Private John G. Noel, Company L, 7th Ohio Cavalry

5th Sergeant Adelbert Noyes, Company G, 9th West Virginia Infantry

Private Andrew Null, Company K, 2nd West Virginia Cavalry

Private Bantalion Nutischer, Company C, 47th Ohio Infantry

Private Michael O'Conner, Company D, 9th West Virginia Infantry

Private Michael O'Shaughnessey/O'Shaughnessy, Company B, 37th Iowa Infantry

Private Robert Oldham, Company H, 44th Ohio Infantry

Private William H. Oliver, Companies E & K, 47th Ohio Infantry

Private Erastus Orcutt, Company E, 34th Massachusetts Infantry

Private Thomas J. Osbern/Osborn/Osburn, Company H, 8th West Virginia Infantry

Private Jefferson Osborn, Companies H & I, 7th West Virginia Cavalry

Private William Osborn/Osburn, Company D, 91st Ohio Infantry

Private George Pack, Company F, 5th West Virginia Infantry

Private James Page, Companies E & K, 47th Ohio Infantry

Private Reuben Page, Company K, 2nd Ohio Cavalry

Private James A. Parker, Company F, 23rd Ohio Infantry

Private Andrew Parson/Parsons, Company D, 91st Ohio Infantry

Private George W./N. Parsons, Company K, 8th Virginia (West Virginia) Infantry & Company M, 7th West Virginia Cavalry

Private Thomas Patten/Patton, Company A, 37th Iowa Infantry

Corporal Hezekiah Patterson, Company C, 13th West Virginia Infantry

Private James A. Patterson, Independent Battery, 1st Ohio Light Artillery & Company H, 7th Veteran Reserve Corps

Private Joshua D. Pauley, Companies L & H, 7th West Virginia Cavalry

Private Washington Pauley, Company M, 7th West Virginia Cavalry

Private John B. Payne, Company D, 91st Ohio Infantry

Private Alonzo Peitzel, Companies A & E, 34th Ohio Infantry

Sergeant Samuel F. Pence, Company M, 11th Pennsylvania Cavalry

Private Joshua B. Perdue, Company B, 44th Ohio Infantry & 8th Ohio Cavalry

Private John Peters, Company B, 37th Ohio Infantry

Corporal William Peterson, Company G, 22nd Kentucky Infantry

Private Peter Petery, Company G, 7th West Virginia Cavalry

Teamster Charles Peyton, Company H, 9th Infantry, West Virginia

Private John Pflum/Plum, Simmonds' Battery, Kentucky Light Artillery

2nd Lt. Thomas Newcomb, Co. F, 7th West Virginia Cavalry. Died at Gallipolis on August 15, 1863 of consumption. Bill Newcomb collection, courtesy of Steve Cunningham.

Private Caleb Phillips, Company A, 7th West Virginia Cavalry

Private James A. Phillips, Company C, 7th West Virginia Cavalry

Private Canaan Pierce, Company E, 13th West Virginia Infantry

Private William Pierce, Company I, 44th Ohio Infantry & 8th Ohio Cavalry

Corporal George W. Pine, Company D, 9th West Virginia Infantry

Corporal James M. Pine, Company K, 2nd West Virginia Cavalry

Private Benjamin N. Piper, Company C, 50th Ohio Infantry, Company F, 99th Ohio Infantry & Company H, 140th Infantry Ohio National Guard

Private James M. Pitchfield/Pitchford/Pitsford/Pittsford, Company K, 13th West Virginia Infantry

Private Lewis Plybon/Plyburn, Company I, 9th West Virginia Infantry & Company D, 1st West Virginia Veteran Infantry

Private James M. Powell, Company K, 2nd West Virginia Cavalry

Private Jacob E. Predmore, Company F, 23rd Ohio Infantry

Private Isaac Price, Company D, 116th Ohio Infantry

Private James Price, Company E, 34th Ohio Infantry

Private Thomas F. Prichard, Company F, 33rd Ohio Infantry

Private Zachariah Priestly, Company C, 13th West Virginia Infantry

Private Samuel N. Proffitt, Company F, 13th West Virginia Infantry

Private Jonas/Jones S. Pruden, Company E, 21st Ohio Infantry, Company K, 14th Ohio Infantry & Company D, 8th Veteran Reserve Corps

Private William T. Pugh, Company E, 9th West Virginia Infantry

2nd Lieutenant Yonathless Pullin, Company K, 9th West Virginia Infantry

Private Fulton G. Quimby, Company G, 36th Ohio Infantry

Private John M. Radcliff, Company H, 2nd West Virginia Cavalry

Private David W. Rainey, Company E, 172nd Infantry, Ohio National Guard

Private John Ramsey, Companies E & F, 98th Ohio Infantry

Private John A. Ramsey, Company E, 89th Ohio Infantry

Private Alfred T. Rand, Trumbull Guards Independent Company, Ohio Infantry

Saddler Jobe Randolph, Company L, 7th Ohio Cavalry, Ohio

Private Jacob C. Rardin, Company F, 2nd West Virginia Cavalry

Private James Ratcliff/Ratliff, Company B, 5th West Virginia Infantry

Corporal Richard Rawling, Companies I & B, 2nd West Virginia Cavalry

Private Samuel Reed, Company K, 2nd West Virginia Cavalry

Private John Reeves, Company E, 34th Ohio Infantry

Private John Reindl/Reindle/Reindel/Rindle, Company I, 37th Ohio Infantry & Company 15, 2nd Battalion Veteran Reserve Corps

Private Gottlieb/Gottliep Rentchler/Renthler, Company G, 8th Ohio Cavalry

Private Patrick H. Reynolds, Company I, 91st Ohio Infantry

Private Joseph F. Rhodes, Company H, 34th Ohio Infantry & 36th Ohio Infantry

Private John Rice, Company G, 91st Ohio Infantry

Private Lyman Richard/Richards, Company D, 75th Illinois Infantry

Private William Richardson, Company G, 91st Ohio Infantry

Private Harrison Richart, Company K, 91st Ohio Infantry

Private Jacob Ridenour/Redenow, Company I, 37th Ohio Infantry

Private William Rider, Companies E & F, 60th Ohio Infantry

Private Jacob Rieger, Company D, 37th Ohio Infantry

Private Jonah Rife, Company G, 1st Ohio Heavy Artillery

Private Ulysses D. Riley, Company D, 23rd Ohio Infantry & 77th Ohio Infantry

Captain Benjamin Roberts, Companies C, A, & B and F & S, 56th Ohio Infantry

Private James Roberts, Company A, 91st Ohio Infantry

Private John B. Roberts, Company A, 9th West Virginia Infantry

Private John C. Roberts, Company B, 5th West Virginia Infantry

Sergeant William Roberts, Company C, 56th Ohio Infantry

1st Lieutenant John W. Rockhold, Company C, 91st Ohio Infantry

Private Allen Robinson, Company C, 2nd West Virginia Infantry

Private Asahel Rogers, Company G, 9th West Virginia Infantry

Private Dudley Rogers, Company B, 23rd Ohio Infantry

Private Wesley M. Rogers, Company F, 98th Ohio Infantry

Private Joseph Rollins, Company E, 2nd West Virginia Cavalry

Sergeant Benjamin Ronk, Company I, 7th West Virginia Cavalry

Private John W. Ropp, Company F, 44th Ohio Infantry & 8th Ohio Cavalry

Private William Rose, Company C, 91st Ohio Infantry

Private William F. Rosenbarger/Rosenbargar/Rosenburger, Companies F, C & E, 34th Ohio Infantry

Private Andrew J. Ross, Company K, 7th West Virginia Cavalry

Private Isaac Roush, Company E, 4th West Virginia Infantry

Private Peter Roush, Company E, 4th West Virginia Infantry

Private Timothy B. Rucker, Company D, 42nd Ohio Infantry

Private John C. Rupe, Company A, 2nd West Virginia Cavalry

Private William Rush/Rust, Company K, 2nd West Virginia Cavalry

Private Philip/Phillip C. Safford, Company Unassigned, 36th Ohio Infantry

Private Samuel B. Sample, Company G, 36th Ohio Infantry

Private Daniel W. Sanders, Company A, 2nd West Virginia Cavalry

Private Henry Sands, Company B, 12th Ohio Infantry

Sergeant Henry D. Sawyer, Companies L & E, 2nd Ohio Cavalry

Private George P. Schaffer/Shafer, Company E, 44th Ohio Infantry & 8th Ohio Cavalry

Private George Schelhas, Company I, 37th Ohio Infantry

Private Casper Schild, Company I, 107th Ohio Infantry

Private Carl Schlagelmillig, Company H, 44th Ohio Infantry & 8th Ohio Cavalry

Sergeant Casper Schmidt/Smith, Company C, 37th Ohio Infantry

Private Christopher Schmidt/Schmith/Smith, Company I, 37th Ohio Infantry & Company F, 124th Ohio Infantry

Sergeant Ferdinand Schwecke/Schwenke, Company G, 47th Ohio Infantry

Private Charles C. Scott, Companies A & K, 2nd West Virginia Cavalry

Private Joel C. Scott, Company E, 92nd Ohio Infantry & Company 66, 2nd Battalion Veteran Reserve Corps (organized at Gallipolis, OH, 1863)

Private Edwin D. Seaman/Seamans, Companies H & B, 47th Ohio Infantry

Private Frank Seaman, Company I, 5th Ohio Infantry & Quartermaster Sergeant, 1st Independent Battery, Ohio Light Artillery

Private Irving W. Searles, Company H, 101st Ohio Infantry

Private Martin Seibel, Company C, 28th Ohio Infantry

Private Jacob Shack, Company K, 12th Ohio Infantry

Private John Shafer/Shaffer, Company A, 34th Ohio Infantry

Private Oliver Shaner, Company A, 31st Ohio Infantry

Private Robert Sharp, Companies H & I, 98th Ohio Infantry & Company 66, 2nd Battalion Veteran Reserve Corps (organized at Gallipolis, OH, 1863)

Private George F. Shea, Company A, 98th Ohio Infantry

Private William M. Shannon, Company G, 4th West Virginia Infantry & Company C, 2nd West Virginia Veteran Infantry

Captain Calvin A. Shepherd, F & S, 4th West Virginia Infantry

Private Levi Shepherd, Company K, 91st Ohio Infantry

Private George T. Shew/Shoe/Shue, Company G, 98th Ohio Infantry

Private William I. Shirley, Company K, 21st Ohio Infantry

Private Samuel Shown, Company I, 13th West Virginia Infantry

Private James H. Shreves/Shrieves, Company C, 2nd Virginia (West Virginia) Cavalry

Private James H. Simmings/Sinnings, Company C, 11th Ohio Infantry

Private Henry Simmons, Company B, 5th West Virginia Infantry

Lieutenant William H.H. Sisson, Company B, 4th West Virginia Infantry

Private John N./W. Skees, Trumbull Guards Independent Company, Ohio Infantry

Private James D. Skinner, Company A, 2nd West Virginia Cavalry

Private Robert S. Slack, Company C, 2nd West Virginia Cavalry

Private George P. Slade, Company A, 44th Ohio Infantry & 8th Ohio Cavalry

Private William Small, Company G, 5th   West Virginia Cavalry & 6th West Virginia Cavalry

Private Alexander Smith, Company F, 91st Ohio Infantry

Private Barney Smith, Companies H & B, 47th Ohio Infantry

Private Clarkson Smith, Companies G & F, 23rd Ohio Infantry

Private Henry L. Smith, Company A & L, 7th West Virginia Cavalry

Private Isaac F. Smith, Company K, 8th Virginia (West Virginia) Infantry & 7th West Virginia Cavalry

Private James Smith, Companies H & B, 47th Ohio Infantry

Private James T. N. Smith, Company B, 34th Ohio Infantry

Private James T. Smith, Company B, 91st Ohio Infantry

Private John Smith, Company F, 13th West Virginia Infantry

Private Joseph Smith, Company B, 37th Iowa Infantry

Private Luke S. Smith, Company D, 13th West Virginia Infantry

Private Rice Smith, Company K, 12th Ohio Infantry

Private Riley H. Smith, Company D, 3rd West Virginia Cavalry

Private Thomas Smith, Company A, McLaughlin's Squadron Ohio Cavalry

Corporal William Smith, Company E, 2nd West Virginia Cavalry

Private William H. Smith, Company D, 8th Virginia (West Virginia) Infantry & 7th West Virginia Cavalry

Private William S. Smith, Company G, 172nd Infantry Ohio National Guard

Private James A. Snedegar, Company K, 7th West Virginia Cavalry

Private Francis Snyder/Snider, Company A, 44th Ohio Infantry & 8th Ohio Cavalry

Private Martin Sowards, Company H, 9th West Virginia Infantry; 1st West Virginia Veteran Infantry; Company D, 3rd West Virginia Cavalry; Company K, 4th West Virginia Cavalry; & Company G, 1st Ohio Heavy Artillery

Private Henry S. Spafford, Company I, 21st Ohio Infantry

Private James Spaulding, Company F, 5th West Virginia Infantry

Private Elifus Spurlock, Company K, 7th West Virginia Cavalry

Sergeant Norman B. Squires, Company F, 10th West Virginia Infantry

Private Mathew Stafford, Company K, 2nd West Virginia Cavalry

Private Ansel C. Staneart/Stanert/Stanneart/Stannart, 6th Independent Battery, Ohio Light Artillery

Archelus Stanley, Private, Company F, 40th Ohio Infantry & Company C, 73rd Ohio Infantry and Corporal, Company H, 141st Ohio Infantry

Private Mitchell St. Onge, Company B, 7th Ohio Infantry

Private Robert R. Starkey, Company A, 5th West Virginia Infantry

Private James State, Company K, 2nd West Virginia Cavalry

Private William H. Staten, Company B, 2nd West Virginia Cavalry

Private John B./R. Steed/Steel, Company C, 13th West Virginia Infantry

Private David Stevenson, Company F, 13th West Virginia Infantry

Corporal James Stewart, Company C, 34th Ohio Infantry

Corporal Michael Stewart, Company E, 92nd Ohio Infantry

Sergeant William C. Stewart, Company E, 22nd Kentucky Infantry

Private Walter Stivers, Company E, 91st Ohio Infantry

Private Melchior Storer, Company B, 37th Ohio Infantry

Private William Stormont, Company M, 7th Ohio Cavalry

Private Harrison Stover, Company H, 8th Virginia (West Virginia) Infantry & 7th West Virginia Cavalry

John W. Stricklan, Private, Co. F, 7th WV Cavalry

Private Nathan J. Strickland, Jr., Company C, 21st Ohio Infantry

Corporal John/Josiah C. Strickler, Company B, 14th Pennsylvania Cavalry

Quartermaster Sergeant William H. Strickler, Company B, 14th Pennsylvania Cavalry

Private Arnold Streum/Streun, Company I, 107th Ohio Infantry

Samuel Sturgeon, Corporal, Co. L, 7th WV Cavalry

William P. Surratt, Sergeant, Co. H, 7th WV Cavalry

Private Thomas H. Sutton, Company I, 34th Ohio Infantry & Company C, 36th Ohio Infantry

Private Hiram W. Swanay/Sweeney, Company K, 4th Tennessee Infantry

Private James C. Switzer, Company B, 173rd Ohio Infantry & Company Unassigned, 183rd Ohio Infantry

Private Charles Tatham, Company D, 16th Ohio Infantry

Private Elmore Taylor, Company K, 13th West Virginia Infantry

Private John W. Taylor, Company I, 91st Ohio Infantry

Private John F. Teel/Tiel, Company A, 13th West Virginia Infantry

Private Samuel Tennell, Ohio State Militia

Corporal Franklin Thacker, Company A, 5th West Virginia Infantry

Private Harrison Thacker, Company H, 13th West Virginia Infantry

Private Ambrose G. Thair, Company I, 123rd Illinois Infantry

Franklin Thomas, Private, Co. E, 7th WV Cavalry

Private John Thomas, Company M, 3rd West Virginia Cavalry

Private John Thomas, Company A, 173rd Ohio Infantry

Private George Thompson, Company I, 21st Ohio Infantry

Private Henry Thompson, Company F, 5th Virginia (West Virginia) Infantry

Private James G. Thornton, Company D, 91st Ohio Infantry

Corporal Thomas Tope, Company G, 140th Ohio Infantry

William A. Trent, Private, Co. L, 7th WV Cavalry

Private Joseph Tritch, Company A, 47th Ohio Infantry

Sergeant David S. Trobridge/Trowbridge, Company G, 4th West Virginia Infantry

Private Jacob W. Tucker, Company D, 13th West Virginia Infantry & Company 66, 2nd Battalion Veteran Reserve Corps (organized at Gallipolis, OH, 1863)

Private William A. Tall/Tull, Company I, 2nd West Virginia Cavalry

Private Dewitt Turner, Company A, 4th West Virginia Infantry

Private Milan Turner, Company E, 2nd West Virginia Cavalry

Private William Turner, Company H, 8th Virginia (West Virginia) Infantry & 7th West Virginia Cavalry

Private William B.P. Turner, Company G, 92nd Ohio Infantry & Company 66, 2nd Battalion Veteran Reserve Corps (organized at Gallipolis, OH, 1863)

Private John Turney/Turrey/Turry, Company A, 11th Virginia (West Virginia) Infantry

Private George Tyler, Company D, 91st Ohio Infantry

Private James Tyler, Company G, 11th West Virginia Infantry

Private George M. Udell, Company B, 23rd Ohio Infantry

Private Joseph H. Ulrey, Company A, 34th Ohio Infantry

Private James W. Vance, Company E, 91st Ohio Infantry

Private Josiah W. Vance, Company G, 4th West Virginia Infantry

Private Frank Vandame, Company A, 47th Ohio Infantry

Private Thomas Vandyne, Company H, 11th Ohio Infantry

Private James Vanhorn, Company D 91st Ohio Infantry & Company 66, 2nd Battalion Veteran Reserve Corps (organized at Gallipolis, OH, 1863)

Private Samuel W. Vanpelt, Company E, 193rd Ohio Infantry

Saddler Charles G. Varian/Varien/Varyan, Companies I & B, 2nd West Virginia Cavalry

Private Peter Voelker, Company I, 37th Ohio Infantry

Private George Volmott, Company A, 37th Iowa Infantry

Private James M. Wagar/Wager, Trumbull Guards Independent Company, Ohio Infantry

Sergeant Herman/Herrman Waldman, Company G, 37th Ohio Infantry

Private John W. Waldron, Company F, 44th Ohio Infantry & 8th Ohio Cavalry

Private Charles S. Walker, Company H, 53rd Ohio Infantry

Private Nathaniel R. Walker, Company L, 2nd West Virginia Cavalry

Sergeant William E./H./W Walker, Company H, 9th Pennsylvania Cavalry

Private James R. Walkup, Company F, 13th West Virginia Infantry

Private James E. Wallace, Company I, 1st West Virginia Infantry

Private George W. Walters, Company A, 121st Ohio Infantry

Private Thomas R. Walters, Company L, 7th Ohio Cavalry

Private William F. Walters, Company F, 92nd Ohio Infantry

Private David S. Wamhoff, Company A, 44th Ohio Infantry & 8th Ohio Cavalry

Corporal Curtis Ward, Company C, 1st Kentucky Infantry

Private Peter Ward, Company E, 4th West Virginia Infantry

Corporal Samuel Ward, Company B, 73rd Ohio Infantry

Private Cornelius Warman, Company H, 2nd West Virginia Cavalry

Private James Wartman/Wortman, Company D, 23rd Ohio Infantry

Private William W. Washburn, Company B, 141st Infantry Ohio National Guard

Private Andrew Watery, Companies B & K, 2nd Ohio Cavalry

Private Daniel L. Watkins, Company F, 84th Indiana Infantry

Private John W. Watson, Company B, 37th Iowa Infantry

Private Thomas Weatherwax, Company A, 20th Iowa Infantry & 37th Iowa Infantry

Private Alfred Weaver, Company I, 40th Ohio Infantry

Private Franz W./H. Weber, Company K, 7th Ohio Infantry

1st Sergeant Henry Weber, Company G, 47th Ohio Infantry

Private Gilbert G. Webster, Company B, 116th Ohio Infantry

Private Horace L. Weeks, Company K, 91st Ohio Infantry

Sergeant William H. Weller, Company C, 54th Pennsylvania Infantry

Private Aaron Whaley/Whaly, Company G, 91st Ohio Infantry

Private Joseph R. Wheeler, Company H, 9th Virginia (West Virginia) Infantry

Corporal Andrew Whitbeck, Company A, 37th Iowa Infantry

Sergeant Asa White, Company F, 91st Ohio Infantry

Lieutenant Adam L. Whitehead, Company K, 1st Tennessee Cavalry

Private Henry Whiteman, Company H 34th Ohio Infantry & Company 66, 2nd Battalion Veteran Reserve Corps (organized at Gallipolis, OH, 1863)

Private George Whitman, Company K, 121st Ohio Infantry

Private James A. Whittington, Company I, 13th West Virginia Infantry

Private William H. Whittington, Company I, 13th West Virginia Infantry

Private Joseph H. Whittlesy, Company F, 4th West Virginia Infantry

Private Hiram Willcox, Jr., Company B, 91st Ohio Infantry

Private John N. Wiley, Company F, 2nd West Virginia Infantry

Private Albert C. Williams, Company I, 53rd Ohio Infantry

Private Enoch Williams, Company B, 4th West Virginia Infantry

Private George Williams, Companies A & E, 11th Ohio Infantry

Private John C. Williams, Company A, 41st Ohio Infantry

Private Matthew F. Williams, Company K, 7th West Virginia Cavalry

Captain Simon Williams, Company D, 13th West Virginia Infantry

Private Charles O. Willis, Company C, 13th West Virginia Infantry

Captain Hambleton Willis, Company E, 5th West Virginia Infantry

1st Lieutenant Edward S. Wilson, Company H, 91st Ohio Infantry

Private Ezekiel H. Wilson, Company B, 13th West Virginia Infantry

Private Ithiel J./S. Wilson, Trumbull Guards Independent Company, Ohio Infantry

Private James Wilson, Company G, 30th Ohio Infantry

Private Thomas Wilson, Company G, 91st Ohio Infantry

Private Jackson A. Winters, Company G, 4th West Virginia Infantry

Private James Wine, Company F, 4th West Virginia Infantry

Private Baron de Kalb Wintz, Company A, 13th West Virginia Infantry

Private Ezra Wise, Company A, 5th West Virginia Infantry

Private Henry D. Wise, Company D, 44th Ohio Infantry & 8th Ohio Cavalry

Private David Wolfe, Company B, 13th West Virginia Infantry & Company 66, 2nd Battalion Veteran Reserve Corps (organized at Gallipolis, OH, 1863)

Private David M. Wood, Company K, 12th Ohio Infantry & Company H, 7th Veteran Reserve Corps

Sergeant Henry F. Wood, Company M, 7th Ohio Cavalry

Private Simon P. Wood, Company C, 2nd Cavalry, West Virginia

Private John R. Woods/Wood, Company G, 60th Ohio Infantry

Private John Woodburn, Company E, 14th West Virginia Infantry

Private Charles M. "Ohio" Woodland, Company G, 60th Ohio Infantry

Private Frank Woodrow, 1st Independent Battery, Ohio Light Artillery

Private Eli Woodward, Company C, 91st Ohio Infantry

Private James L. Woodyard, Company C, 13th West Virginia Infantry

Private George Worrall/Worrell, Company B, 37th Iowa Infantry

Sergeant Benjamin S. Wright, Company F, 36th Ohio Infantry

Private John Yeisley, Independent Battery, 1st Ohio Light Artillery

Private Benjamin Yeauger, Company G, 116th Ohio Infantry

Private William B. Yauger, Company G, 116th Ohio Infantry

Private David K. Young, Company I, 13th West Virginia Infantry

Private John Young, Company K, 49th Indiana Infantry

Private Samuel H. Young, Companies B & I, 2nd West Virginia Cavalry

Private Jacob Zeigler, Company H, 20th Ohio Infantry and 2nd Lieutenant, 1st Independent Battery, Ohio Light Artillery

Private George F. Zeller, Company D, 12th Ohio Infantry

Private Mathias Zeitler, Company G, 12th Ohio Infantry

Private Stephen/Stephan Zuercher/Zurcher, Company A, 37th Ohio Infantry

APPENDIX E

Confederate Soldiers Associated with the USAGH Gallipolis, Ohio

There were likely more Confederate soldiers treated at the U.S. Army Hospital in Gallipolis than are listed here. These soldiers were captured at the Battle of Lewisburg, Virginia, which was fought on May 23, 1862. At least seven of these soldiers were wounded and taken first to the U.S. Army hospital at Charleston, Virginia, and then transported to Gallipolis. A number of the recuperated survivors were sent to Wheeling's Atheneum Prison and, subsequently, to Camp Chase Prison in Columbus, Ohio.

Four soldiers who died at the hospital are buried in Gallipolis' Pine Street Cemetery in marked graves: Private Robert James Thrasher, Private James H.W. McKinney, Private Adam Rader, and Private William Z. Wickline.

Captain William F. Bahlmann, Company K, 22nd Virginia Infantry

Private Elisha Barbour, Company A, 50th Virginia Infantry

Private William T. Chandler, Company D, 26th Battalion Virginia Infantry

Private Ralph/Rafe/Rufus Elkins, Company I, 50th Virginia Infantry

Private William T. Hansbarger/Hansberger, Company D, 26th Battalion Virginia Infantry

Private Andrew J. Hicks/Hix, Company B, 22nd Virginia Infantry

Private Alvin/Alvis S. Marshall, Company I, 50th Virginia Infantry

Private Joseph Nathan Marshall, Company I, 50th Virginia Infantry

Private James H.W. McKinney, Company G, 22nd Virginia Infantry

Private George McKnight, Company G, 22nd Virginia Infantry

Private John Wesley Mitchell, Company I, 50th Infantry, Virginia

Private Augustus Morris/Morse, Company E, 26th Battalion Virginia Infantry, & 108th Virginia Militia

Private Patrick H. Murray, Company K, 22nd Virginia Infantry

Private Wilson Neighbors, Company K, 22nd Virginia Infantry

Private Jesse Nichols, Company I, 50th Virginia Infantry

Private Adam Rader, Company B, 22nd Virginia Infantry

Private Christopher Rhodes/Rhoads, Company D, 22nd Virginia Infantry

Private James Calvin Smith, Company I, 50th Virginia Infantry

Private John C. Smith, Company E, 2nd Virginia Artillery & 22nd Virginia Infantry

Private John O. Smith, Company A, 22nd Virginia Infantry

Private William L. Smith, Company I, 50th Virginia Infantry

Private Preston Snow, Company I, 50th Virginia Infantry

Private George A./L. Stull, Company A, 22nd Virginia Infantry

Private William J. "Bill" Taylor, Company K, 22nd Virginia Infantry

Private Robert James Thrasher, Company I, 50th Virginia Infantry

Private John Thomas White, Company E, 26th Battalion Virginia Infantry

Private William Z. Wickline, Company B, Lemons' & McNeer's Virginia Battalions, 108th Virginia Militia & Company Unassigned, 50th Virginia Infantry

SELECTED BIBLIOGRAPHY

Almanacs

Childs, George W. and McKean, William V., *The national almanac and annual record for the year 1864*. Philadelphia, PA: George W. Childs, 1864. Internet Archive electronic e-book: https://archive.org/details/nationalalmana-ca00mcke/page/n3/mode/2up/search/Medical+Department+U.S.+Volunteers?q=Medical+Department+U.S.+Volunteers

The American Almanac and Repository of Useful Knowledge for the Year 1860. Boston, MA: Crosby, Nichols, and Company; London, Eng.: Trubner and Co.; Paris, Fr: Hector Bossange, 1860. Internet Archive e-book: https://archive.org/details/B-001-001-680/page/n5/mode/2up

Biographies

Banta, John Quincy Adams, *A Frisian Family: The Banta Genealogy*, Theodore Melvin Banta, author, p. 293. New York, NY: Publisher not identified, 1893.

Gabriel, Jonas Frank, M.D., Miami County, Ohio Genealogical Researchers Biography Index. Web page: http://www.thetroyhistoricalsociety.org/Stories/Biograph/biog-fl/1267.htm

Gabriel, Jonas Frank, M.D., *A history of the Gabriel family of southern Pennsylvania and their descendants*, p. 24, 1960. Internet Archive e-book: https://archive.org/details/historyofgabriel00sham/page/n43/mode/2up/search/Jonas+Frank+Gabriel

Harper, James, Captain, *Death of Capt. James Harper*, obituary, *Gallipolis Bulletin*, September 22, 1891. Gallia Genealogical Society web page: http://www.galliagenealogy.org/Civil%20War/CW_obits/cwobits_h-l.htm#JamesHarper

Hayes, Rutherford B., Major, 23rd Ohio Volunteer Infantry; former U.S. Congressman; former Ohio Governor; Nineteenth U.S. President. Rutherford B. Hayes Presidential Library and Museums at Spiegel Grove, OH. Web page: https://www.rbhayes.org/hayes/biography/

Noble, David, M.D., *The biographical encyclopaedia of Ohio of the nineteenth century*, p. 301. *Making of America* digital library page: https://quod.lib.umich.edu/m/moa/AHU5132.0001.001/419

Robison, James Dickey, M.D., Find a Grave Memorial, https://www.findagrave.com/memorial/58861338

Thrasher, Robert, Private, 22nd Virginia C.S.A., Find a Grave Memorial, https://www.findagrave.com/memorial/14869244

Wittenmyer, Annie Turner, *Encyclopedia Britannica Online*, https://www.britannica.com/biography/Annie-Turner-Wittenmyer

Blog posts

Campbell, William T., Ed.D., R.N., "The Innovative Design of Civil War Pavilion Hospitals," National Museum of Civil War Medicine website, Surgeon's Call blog, posted February 20th, 2018. Blog post: https://www.civilwarmed.org/pavilion-hospitals/

Cirillo, Frank, "'The Iron Arm of the Black Man': The Long Road to African American Military Service, Part II," John L. Nau III Center for Civil War History, University of Virginia, posted January 27, 2020. Blog post: https://naucenter.as.virginia.edu/blog-page/1166

Dannehl, Katherine, "Dr. Lincoln R. Stone, Civil War Surgeon," The Beehive blog, Massachusetts Historical Society, updated on August 4, 2017. Blog post: http://www.masshist.org/beehiveblog/2017/08/dr-lincoln-r-stone-civil-war-surgeon/

Densford, Daryl, Chaplain, "Civil War Hospital Chaplains," The Chaplain Kit Online Museum. Blog post: https://thechaplainkit.com/chaplains/non-combat-ministry/hospitals/civil-war-hospitals/

Diaz, Ashley, "Little Women in the Civil War," Pieces of History blog, National Archives, November 29, 2011. Blog post: https://prologue.blogs.archives.gov/2011/11/29/little-women-in-the-civil-war/

Dorwart, Dr. Bonnie Brice, "Civil War Hospitals," Essential Civil War Curriculum, Virginia Center for Civil War Studies at Virginia Tech. Blog post: https://www.essentialcivilwarcurriculum.com/civil-war-hospitals.html

Eash, Codie, "A Scene Not Easily Forgotten': The U.S. Christian Commission at Antietam," National Museum of Civil War Medicine, posted April 24th, 2020. Blog post: https://www.civilwarmed.org/christian-commission-antietam/

Harbor, Stark, "Dorothea Dix," National Museum of Civil War Medicine website, Surgeon's Call blog, posted March 14th, 2016. Blog post: https://www.civilwarmed.org/dorothea-dix/

Hicks, Robert, Director, Mütter Museum & the Historical Medical Library, "Full diet or half diet?". *Fugitive Leaves*, blog of The Historical Medical Library of the

College of Physicians of Philadelphia, March 2, 2017. Blog post: http://histmed.collegeofphysicians.org/full-diet-or-half-diet/

Lively, Matthew W., "J.E. Hanger Lost His Leg But Not His Ingenuity," Civil War Profiles blog, posted March 16, 2013. Blog post: https://www.civilwarprofiles.com/j-e-hanger-lost-his-leg-but-not-ingenuity/

Slawson, Robert, M.D., F.A.C.R., "The Development of Triage," National Museum of Civil War Medicine website, *Surgeon's Call* blog, posted June 7, 2014. Blog post: https://www.civilwarmed.org/surgeons-call/triage1/

Weitz, Mark A., "Desertion, Cowardice and Punishment," Essential Civil War Curriculum, Virginia Center for Civil War Studies at Virginia Tech. Blog post: https://www.essentialcivilwarcurriculum.com/desertion,-cowardice-and-punishment.html

White, Jonathan W., "How Lincoln Won the Soldier Vote," *Disunion* blog, part of *Opinionator, The New York Times,* published November 7, 2014. Blog post: https://web.archive.org/web/20200212221724/https://opinionator.blogs.nytimes.com/2014/11/07/how-lincoln-won-the-soldier-vote/

Williams, Rachel, "Civil War Chaplains," National Museum of Civil War Medicine website, *Surgeon's Call* blog, posted February 5, 2017. Web post: https://www.civilwarmed.org/chaplains/

Books and Booklets

Bahlmann, William F., and Abbot, Rob, *Down in the Ranks or Bread and Blankets.* Arlington, VA: Publisher not identified, 1970.

Barnes, Joseph K.; Huntington, D.L.; Otis, George A.; Smart, Charles; Woodward, Joseph J., Contributors, *The Medical and Surgical History of the War of the Rebellion*, Volumes 1 through 6, United States Surgeon General's Office. Washington, D.C.: Government Printing Office, 1870-1888. National Library of Medicine e-books: https://collections.nlm.nih.gov/catalog/nlm:nlmuid-14121350R-mvset

Barr, R.N., Surgeon General of Ohio, *Annual Report of the Surgeon General to the Governor of the State of Ohio.* Columbus, OH: Richard Nevins, 1866.

Blackman, George C. and Tripler, Charles S., *Handbook for the Military Surgeon.* Cincinnati: Robert Clarke and Co, 1861. National Library of Medicine e-book: https://collections.nlm.nih.gov/bookviewer?PID=nlm:nlmuid-46920320R-bk#page/2/mode/2up/search/hospital

Brayton, Mary Clark and Terry, Ellen F., *Our acre and its harvest: Historical sketch of the Soldiers' Aid Society of Northern Ohio*, Cleveland Branch of the United States Sanitary Commission. Cleveland, OH: Fairbanks, Benedict & Co., 1869. Internet e-pub: https://archive.org/details/ouracreanditsha00terrgoog/page/n456/mode/2up/search/Post+Hospital+Gallipolis?q=Post+Hospital+Gallipolis

Chernow, Ron, *Grant.* New York: Penguin Press, 2017.

Cox, Jacob Dolson, A.M., L.L.D., *Military Reminiscences of the Civil War, Volume I, April 1861-November 1863.* New York, NY: Charles Scribner's Sons, 1900. Internet Archive e-book: https://archive.org/details/militaryreminiscen01cox-drich/page/n9/mode/2up/search/Confederate+Gallipolis?q=Confederate+Gallipolis

Dee, Christine, Editor, *Ohio's War: The Civil War in Documents.* Athens, OH: Ohio University Press, 2006.

Eaton, J.H., Paymaster, U.S. Army, The Army Paymaster's Manual, or Collection of Official Rules. Washington, D.C.: Government Printing Office, 1864. Google e-book: https://books.google.com/books?id=eHcDAAAAYAAJ&pg=PA91&lpg=PA91&dq=1864+hospital+chaplain+pay+raise&source=bl&ots=WZ2mzdeL8q&sig=ACfU3U0Ak_9Z3sG8IQ7JozGfrgBZgDT-Bw&hl=en&sa=X&ved=2ahUKEwjx7-Wx_MnoAhXskOAKHYsvD_UQ6AEwAHoECAsQKQ#v=onepage&q=1864%20hospital%20chaplain%20pay%20raise&f=false

Freemon, Frank R., *Gangrene and Glory: Medical Care During the American Civil War.* Urbana and Chicago, IL: University of Illinois Press, 1998.

Gillett, Mary C., *The Army Medical Department, 1818-1865.* Center of Military History, United States Army, Washington, D.C., 1987. Internet Archive e-book: https://archive.org/details/TheArmyMedicalDepartment18181865/page/n1/mode/2up/search/%22U.S.+Army+General+Hospital+Gallipolis%22?q=%22U.S.+Army+General+Hospital+Gallipolis%22

Haber, Barbara, *From Hardtack to Homefries: An Uncommon History of American Cooks and Meals.* New York, NY: The Free Press, a division of Simon & Schuster, Inc., 2002.

Hamilton, Frank Hastings, M.D., *A Treatise on Military Surgery and Hygiene.* London, Eng.: H. Bailliere; Melbourne, Au.: F. Bailliere; Paris, Fr.: J.Bailliere Et Fils; Madrid, Sp.: C. Bailly-Bailliere, 1865.

Hoff, John V.R., Captain, Medical Department, U.S. Army, *Notes on Bearer Drill with Hand-Litter, Ambulance-Wagon, Etc., Supplementary to a Provisional Manual of Instruction for the Hospital Corps, U.S.A., and Company Bearers.* Fort Reno, Indian Territory (now OK): Publisher not identified, 1889.

Kaminski, Theresa, *Dr. Mary Walker's Civil War: One Woman's Journey to the Medal of Honor and the Fight for Women's Rights.* Lanham, MD: The Rowman & Littlefield Publishing Group, Inc, 2020.

Logan, John A. and Logan, Mary Simmerson Cunningham, *The Part Taken by Women in American History.* Wilmington, DE: The Perry-Nalle Publishing Company, 1912. Google e-book: https://books.google.com/books?id=hnIEAAAAYAAJ&dq=dix%20dame%20%22army%20nurses%20association%22&pg=PA358#v=onepage&q=Hannah%20Maxon&f=false

Lonn, Ella, Ph.D., *Desertion During the Civil War.* New York, NY and London, Eng.: The Century Co., 1928. Hathitrust e-book: https://babel.hathitrust.org/cgi/pt?id=uc1.$b61319&view=1up&seq=11

McKinley, William; Taylor, Samuel M.; Howe, James C., *Official roster of the soldiers of the state of Ohio in the War of the Rebellion, 1861-1866.* Cincinnati, OH: The Ohio Valley Pub. & Mfg. Co, 1886-1895. Internet Archive e-book: https://archive.org/details/ohiowarroster03howerich/page/n6/mode/2up

Memorial R.G.S. [Robert Gould Shaw], Cambridge, MA: Cambridge University Press, 1864. Internet Archive e-book: https://archive.org/details/memorialrgsrober00cambuoft/page/195/mode/1up/search/Lincoln+R.+Stone?q=Lincoln+R.+Stone

Miller, Richard F., Editor, *States at War: A Reference Guide for Ohio in the Civil War, Volume 5.* Lebanon, NH: University Press of New England, 2015.

Moore, Frank, *Women of the war: their heroism and self-sacrifice.* Hartford, CT: S.S. Scranton & Co.; Chicago, IL: R.C. Treat; San Francisco, CA: H.H. Bancroft & Co; Cincinnati, OH: National Publishing Company, 1866. Internet Archive e-book: https://archive.org/details/b24849947/page/n5/mode/2up/search/%22special+diet+kitchen%22?q=%22special+diet+kitchen%22

Moss, Reverend Lemuel, *Annals of the United States Christian Commission.* Philadelphia, PA: J.B. Lippincott & Co, 1868. Internet Archive e-book: https://archive.org/details/annalsofunitedst00moss/page/n9/mode/2up/search/%22special+diet+kitchen%22?q=%22special+diet+kitchen%22

Nightingale, Florence, *Notes on Hospitals.* London, Eng.: Longman, Green, Longman, Roberts and Green, 1863. Google e-book: https://play.google.com/store/books/details?id=2Xu3ZR4UMdEC&rdid=book-2Xu3ZR4UMdEC&rdot=1

Peirpoint, Francis P., Brigadier General, Adjutant General, West Virginia, *Annual Reports of the Adjutant General, and Quarter-Master General, of the State of West Virginia.* Wheeling, WV: John Frew, 1866. Internet Archive e-book: https://archive.org/details/annualreportsofa00west/page/n7/mode/2up/search/Post+Hospital+Gallipolis?q=Post+Hospital+Gallipolis

Reid, Whitelaw, *Ohio in the War: Her Statesmen, Her Generals, and Soldiers, Volume I: History of the State During the War, and the Lives of Her Generals.* Cincinnati, OH: Moore, Wilstach & Baldwin, 1868. E-book: https://brittle-books.library.illinois.edu/brittlebooks_open/Books2009-10/reidwh0001ohiin/reidwh0001ohiinv00001/reidwh0001ohiinv00001_ocr.txt

Rodenbough, Theo. F., Brevet Brigadier General U.S.A. and Haskin, William L., Major, First Artillery, *The Army of the U.S.: Historical Sketches of Staff and Line with Portraits of Generals-in-Chief.* New York, NY: Maynard, Merrill & Co., 1896. U.S. Army Center of Military History e-book: https://history.army.mil/books/R&H/R&H-FM.htm

Schouler, William, *A history of Massachusetts in the Civil War.* Boston, MA: E.P. Dutton & Co., 1868. Internet Archive e-book: https://archive.org/details/historyofmassach00scho/page/n3/mode/2up/search/Lincoln+R.+Stone

Schultz, Jane E., *Women at the Front: Hospital Workers in Civil War America.* Chapel Hill and London: The University of North Carolina Press, 2004.

Smith, George Winston, *Medicines for the Union Army: The United States Army Laboratories During the Civil War.* Madison, WI: American Institute of the History of Pharmacy, 1962. Hathitrust e-book: https://babel.hathitrust.org/cgi/pt?id=mdp.39015020608421&view=1up&seq=5

Strait, N.A., Compiler, *Roster of All Regimental Surgeons and Assistant Surgeons in the Late War, With Their Service, and Last-Known Post Office Address.* Publisher not identified, 1882.

Taylor, Lenette S., *"The Supply for Tomorrow Must Not Fail": The Civil War of Captain Simon Perkins, Jr. a Union Quartermaster.* Kent, OH and London, Eng.: The Kent State University Press, 2004.

Tripler, Charles Stuart, and Blackman, George Curtis. *Handbook for the Military Surgeon: Being a Compendium of the Duties of the Medical Officer in the Field, the Sanitary Management of the Camp, the Preparation of Food, Etc.; with Forms for the Requisitions for Supplies, Returns, Etc.; the Diagnosis and Treatment of Camp Dysentery; and All the Important Points in War Surgery; Including Gunshot Wounds, Amputation, Wounds of the Chest, Abdomen, Arteries and Head, and the Use of Chloroform.* United States: R. Clarke, 1861. Google e-book: https://play.google.com/store/books/details?id=S3Y-AAAAIAAJ&rdid=book-S3Y-AAAAIAAJ&rdot=1

United States Christian Commission, *Information for Army Meetings.* Philadelphia, PA: James B. Rodgers, June and July 1864. Internet Archive e-book: https://archive.org/details/unitedstateschri00slun/page/n5/

mode/2up/search/%22special+diet+kitchen%22?q=%22special+diet+kitc hen%22

Wilder, Theodore, *The History of Company C, Seventh Regiment, O.V.I.*. Oberlin, OH: J.B.T. Marsh, 1866. Google e-book: https://books.google.com/books?id=H-pZBAAAAYAAJ&pg=PA52&lpg=PA52&dq=%22James+R.+Bell%22+physician+Gallipolis,+Ohio&source=bl&ots=MBWKePWqxT&sig=ACfU3U0UQVYBWYRb mJotNeGj-p7nwJxv1A&hl=en&sa=X&ved=2ahUKEwj32fqTxezkAhVJTt8KHU0 DBAkQ6AEwCnoECAkQAQ#v=onepage&q=%22James%20R.%20Bell%22%20 physician%20Gallipolis%2C%20Ohio&f=false

Woodward, Joseph J., *The hospital steward's manual for the instruction of hospital stewards, wardmasters, and attendants, in their several duties*. Philadelphia, PA: J.B. Lippincott & Co, 1863.

Catalogs

Catalogue of the Officers and Students of the Ohio Wesleyan University, for the Academical Year 1852-53, Delaware, Ohio. Cincinnati, OH: The Methodist Book Concern, 1853. Google e-book: https://books.google.com/books?id=gaE4AAAAMAAJ&pg=RA3-PA38&lpg=RA3-PA38&dq=%22Ohio+Wesle yan+University%22+1858&source=bl&ots=caybp1u9-X&sig=ACfU3U06kJYs6B-8dxmjaWF1TvWZJM4kgiA&hl=en&sa=X&ved=2ahUKEwipp8XgxsLoAhV0lnIEHY 9kBYQQ6AEwBXoECAoQAQ#v=onepage&q&f=false

Databases

Ancestry.com

Digital Archives of Bossard Memorial Library, Gallia County District Library: http://bossardlibrary.advantage-preservation.com/

Familysearch.com

Newspapers.com

OhioLINK, OH-TECH Consortium, Ohio.gov: https://www.ohiolink.edu/

Diaries

Hayes, Rutherford B., *Diary and Letters of Rutherford Birchard Hayes, Nineteenth President of the United States, Vol. II, 1861-1865*. Columbus, OH: F.J. Heer, 1922. Google e-book: https://books.google.com/books?id=JxwQAAAAYAA-J&pg=PP13&lpg=PP13&dq=%22ADVANCE+AND+RETREAT--WEST+VIRGINIA--SPRING+OF+1862%22&source=bl&ots=Xb_PRfPBGr&sig=ACfU3U1h-j1y8lEWt0 7EtENkVwhvIhtU3w&hl=en&sa=X&ved=2ahUKEwjC5pTwzffoAhVzhXIEHckqCX YQ6AEwAHoECAYQKQ#v=onepage&q&f=false

Salter, William, "Forty Days with the Christian Commission: A Diary by William Salter," *Iowa Journal of History and Politics*. Iowa City, IA: The State Historical Society of Iowa, 1935.

Digital Collections

Civil War gallery, National Museum of Health and Medicine Collections: https://www.medicalmuseum.mil/index.cfm?p=collections.archives.galleries.index

Lunbeck, Joseph R., Civil War papers, 1861-1864. Virginia Military Institute Archives Digital Collections: http://digitalcollections.vmi.edu/digital/collection/p15821coll11/id/3424/rec/1

Library of Congress *Chronicling America*: loc.gov

Ohio Memory, Newspapers, a collaborative program of the Ohio History Connection and the Library of Ohio. https://ohiomemory.ohiohistory.org/newspapers

The Florence Nightingale Digitization Project, Howard Gotlieb Archival Research Center, Boston University, Boston, MA. http://hgar-srv3.bu.edu/web/florence-nightingale/home

Steamboats in the Great Kanawha River, Steamboat Ledgers and Logbooks Collection, University of Missouri St. Louis Mercantile Library, Pott Library Special Collections. https://umsl.edu/mercantile/collections/pott-library-special-collections/collections/pott21-kanawha-steamboats.html

Wilbur H. Siebert Underground Railroad Collection, Ohio History Connection: https://www.ohiomemory.org/digital/collection/siebert/search

Directories

Wiggins & Weaver's Ohio River Directory for 1871-72, First Issue. Cleveland, OH: Fairbanks, Benedict & Co. 1871.

Dissertations and Theses

Jones, Gregory R., "They Fought the War Together: Southeastern Ohio's Soldiers and Their Families During the Civil War," (2013), Doctorate Dissertation, Kent State University. Online paper: https://etd.ohiolink.edu/!etd.send_file?accession=kent1384347676&disposition=inline

Metheny, Hannah, "'For A Woman': The Fight for Pensions for Civil War Army Nurses" (2013). Undergraduate Honors Theses. Paper 573. https://scholarworks.wm.edu/honorstheses/573

Essays

Coddington, Ronald S., historian and editor, *Military Images* magazine, "Carrie Wilkins Pollard: Working the Special Diet Kitchen," Library of Congress, Prints

& Photographs, Research Guides: https://guides.loc.gov/civil-war-soldiers/carrie-pollard

Genealogical Records

Herrmann, Teresa, Collector/Transcriber, Physicians, Dentists, Midwives and Nurses of Gallia County, Ohio. Gallia County Genealogical Society, OGS Chapter, Inc. Web page: http://www.galliagenealogy.org/medical.htm

Orr, Joyce Whitehead, "Adam L. Whitehead, My G-G-Grandfather," from Index of Taylor families/Whitehead. Web page: http://iagenweb.org/taylor/families/whitehead/Adam_S.html

Histories

History of Gallia County: Containing a Condensed History of the County; Biographical Sketches; General Statistics; Miscellaneous Matters, &c. Chicago, IL and Toledo, OH: H.H. Hardesty & Co, 1882. Hathitrust e-book: https://babel.hathitrust.org/cgi/pt?id=osu.32435061712832&view=1up&seq=3

Journals: Education

Henkle, W.D., Editor, *The Ohio Educational Monthly and The National Teacher: A Journal of Education*, Organ of the Ohio Teachers' Association, Third Series, Volume VI. Salem, OH: W.D. Henkle, 1881. Google e-journal: https://play.google.com/store/books/details?id=eiMbAQAAIAAJ&rdid=book-eiMbAQAAIAAJ&rdot=1

Journals: Historical

Boone, Nancy E. and Sherman, Michael, "Designed to Cure: Civil War Hospitals in Vermont," *Vermont History*, the Proceedings of the Vermont Historical Society, Vol. 69, Nos. 1 & 2, Winter/Spring 2001. Online article: https://vermonthistory.org/journal/69/vt691_204.pdf

Winther, Oscar Osburn, "The Soldier Vote in the Election of 1864," *New York History*, Vol. 25, No.4, October 1944, pp. 440-458. Cooperstown, NY: Fenimore Art Museum. Online article: https://www.jstor.org/stable/23148753?read-now=1&refreqid=excelsior%3A20930d0fdc62a2a51f79f843c8d6d798&seq=19#metadata_info_tab_contents

Journals: Medical

Blaisdell, F W. "Medical advances during the Civil War." Archives of surgery (Chicago, Ill. : 1960) vol. 123,9 (1988): 1045-50. doi:10.1001/archsurg.1988.01400330021001

Bollet, Alfred Jay. "The major infectious epidemic diseases of Civil War soldiers." *Infectious disease clinics of North America* vol. 18,2 (2004): 293-309, table of contents. doi:10.1016/j.idc.2004.01.008

Egenes, Karen J., R.N., Ed.D, "Nursing during the U.S. Civil War: a movement toward the professionalization of nursing," *Hektoen International Journal.* Chicago, IL: Hektoen Institute of Medicine, Winter 2009. Online article: https://hekint.org/2017/02/24/nursing-during-the-us-civil-war-a-movement-toward-the-professionalization-of-nursing-2/#:~:text=Nursing%20during%20the%20US%20Civil%20War%3A%20a,toward%20the%20professionalization%20of%20nursing&text=At%20the%20outbreak%20of%20the,a%20typical%20feminine%20role%20assignment.&text=Another%20group%20interested%20in%20the,the%20Army%20physicians%20and%20surgeons.

Lupton, Ella G., M.D., "History of Medicine in Gallia County, Ohio," article in the *Ohio State Medical Journal,* Columbus, OH: Ohio State Medical Association, 1950. Internet Archive journal: https://archive.org/details/ohiostatemedical4611ohio/page/142/mode/2up

Journals: National Association of Civil War Army Nurses

In Honor of the National Association of Civil War Army Nurses. Atlantic City, New Jersey: Citizens Executive Committee. Hathitrust e-journal: https://catalog.hathitrust.org/Record/000424333

Journals: Woman's Relief Corps

Journal of the Thirteenth Annual Convention of the Woman's Relief Corps, Auxiliary to the Grand Army of the Republic, Louisville, KY, September 12th, 13th and 14th, 1895. Boston, Massachusetts: E.B. Stillings & Co., 1895.

Journal of the Twenty-Eighth National Convention of the Woman's Relief Corps, Auxiliary to the Grand Army of the Republic, Atlantic City, NJ, September 21, 22 and 23, 1910. Boston, Massachusetts: Griffith-Stillings Press, 1910.

Unofficial Proceedings in Connection with the Thirty-Eighth National Encampment, Grand Army of the Republic, held in Boston, week August 15-20, 1904. Boston, Massachusetts: Griffith-Stillings Press, 1907.

Journals: Women

Schultz, Jane E., "The Inhospitable Hospital: Gender and Professionalism in Civil War Medicine," article in *Signs: Journal of Women in Culture and Society.* Chicago, IL: University of Chicago Press, Winter 1992. Article in JSTOR Digital Library: https://www.jstor.org/stable/3174468?read-now=1&seq=1#page_scan_tab_contents

Letters and Official Correspondence

Correspondence and orders from the U.S. Army General Hospital, Gallipolis, OH. 1864-65. Box 1 of 1. Found at NIH/National Library of Medicine Historical Medical Collection. Call letter MSC24.

Hayes, Rutherford B., Letter to Brigadier General C.P. Buckingham, Assistant Adjutant General, on behalf of 23rd O.V.I. Chaplain Russell G. French, May 12, 1862, written from Camp at Mouth of East River, Giles County, Virginia. Online summary of correspondence: https://resources.ohiohistory.org/onlinedoc/civil-war/sa0147/new/33_08.php

Johnson, William Parker, M.D., Letters, 1861-1864, Civil War Correspondence Collection, Ohio University Libraries Digital Archival Collections: https://media.library.ohio.edu/digital/search/searchterm/william%20parker%20johnson%20letters%20(mss%20173)!William%20Parker%20Johnson/field/relatig!all/mode/exact!all/conn/and!and/order/nosort/ad/desc

Salter, Dr. Francis, Post Surgeon, Charleston, Virginia, Letter to Mrs. B. Rouse, Oct. 15, 1861, found online in Report of the Soldiers' Aid Society, of Cleveland, Ohio, and its auxiliaries: to the U.S. Sanitary Commission, at Washington, November 30, 1861. Cleveland, OH: Fairbanks, Benedict Co., 1861.

Stone, Dr. Lincoln R., Surgeon in Charge, U.S. Army General Hospital, Gallipolis, Ohio. Letters received by Surgeon Lincoln R. Stone, 1864. National Archives and Records Administration. 243 pages, downloaded December 2019.

Wickerham, Jacob F., Diary and Account Book, March 18 to June 24, 1865, Civil War Correspondence Collection, Ohio University Libraries Digital Archival Collections: https://media.library.ohio.edu/digital/collection/p15808coll6/id/4896

Magazines

Campbell, William T., Ed.D., R.N., "Overworked, Undermanned and Indispensable: Hospital stewards in the Civil War," *Military Images* magazine, pp.52-56, Autumn 2018. Online article: https://militaryimages.atavist.com/hospital-stewards-in-the-civil-war-autumn-2018

Rector, Charles R., "Morgan 'Goes A-Raiding' and Views West Virginia," *West Virginia Review*, May 1929. West Virginia Archives and History online article: http://www.wvculture.org/history/civilwar/buffington01.html

Manuals

Red Book, A Manual Containing the Rules and Regulations of the Woman's Relief Corps, Auxiliary to the Grand Army of the Republic, and Official Decisions of the

Several National Conventions, with Notes and Explanations by Annie Wittenmyer, Corps. No. 2, W.R.C., Philadelphia, PA, Past National President Woman's Relief Corps. Boston, MA: E.B. Stillings & Co, 1897.

Microform

United States, National Archives and Records Service; United States War Department; United States Office of Commissary General of Prisoners. *Selected records of the War Department relating to Confederate prisoners of war, 1861-1865.* Internet Archive digitized microfilm: https://archive.org/details/selectedrecordso0022unit/page/n1/mode/2up

Military Records

Barnes, Joseph K. and Greenleaf, Charles R., *A manual for the medical officers of the United States Army.* Philadelphia, PA: J.B. Lippincott & Co., 1864. Internet Archive e-pub: https://archive.org/details/62510520R.nlm.nih.gov/page/n3/mode/2up

Grace, William, *The Army Surgeon's Manual for the use of Medical Officers, Cadets, Chaplains, and Hospital Stewards.* New York, NY: Bailliere Brothers, 1864. Internet Archive e-pub: https://archive.org/details/62510300R.nlm.nih.gov/mode/2up

Hammond, William A. and Smith, Joseph R., *Instructions for medical inspectors of the United States Army*, U.S. Surgeon General's Office, Washington, D.C., 1863. Internet Archive e-pub: https://archive.org/details/101533388.nlm.nih.gov/mode/2up

Official Army Register of the Volunteer Force of the United States Army for the Years 1861, '62,' '63, '64, '65, Part IV. Adjutant General's Office, United States, 1865. Hathitrust e-books: https://catalog.hathitrust.org/Record/012288392

Otis, George A., Assistant Surgeon and Brevet Lieutenant Colonel, U.S. Army, *A Report on Amputations at the Hip-Joint in Military Surgery.* Washington, D.C.: Government Printing Office, 1867. Google e-book: https://play.google.com/store/books/details?id=cTkAAAAAQAAJ&rdid=book-cTkAAAAAQAAJ&rdot=1

Ramsey, Frank A., *Hospital Organization of the Department.* Confederate States of America, Army, Knoxville, TN: Headquarters, Department of East Tennessee.

Roll of Honor: names of soldiers who died in defence of the American Union, interred in the National Cemeteries, v. 26. Washington, D.C.: Government Printing Office, 1871. Family Search e-pub: https://www.familysearch.org/library/books/records/item/346093-redirection

Sickness and mortality of the Army during the first year of the war, U.S. Surgeon General's Office, 1863. Internet Archive e-pub: https://archive.org/details/0254775.nlm.nih.gov/page/n17/mode/2up

The War of the Rebellion: A Compilation of the Official Records of the Union and Confederate Armies (alternate title: *Official Records of the Union and Confederate Armies*). Washington, D.C.: Government Printing Office, 1880-1901. Making of America digital archive, Cornell University Library e-books: http://collections.library.cornell.edu/moa_new/waro.html

Newspaper articles

Harper, Roberts S., "Gallipolis, at Outbreak of Civil War, Was Backdoor Step to South; Played Wartime Role That Had No Counterpart," *Gallia Times*, Gallipolis, OH, Saturday, May 27th, 1961, p. 7. Bossard Library Digital Archives. Online article: http://bossardlibrary.advantage-preservation.com/viewer/?k=camp%20carrington&i=f&d=01011890-12312019&m=between&ord=k1&fn=gallia_times_usa_ohio_gallipolis_19610527_english_7&df=1&dt=10

Locher, Paul, "Robison was part of several firsts at start of Civil War," *The Daily Record*, Wooster, OH, May 14, 2008. Online article: https://www.the-daily-record.com/news/20080514/robison-was-part-of-several-firsts-at-start-of-civil-war

Newberry, Dr. J.S., Department Secretary, "Report of the Western Department," *The Sanitary Reporter*, Louisville, KY, September 15, 1863. Hathitrust online article: https://babel.hathitrust.org/cgi/pt?id=hvd.32044103002572&view=1up&seq=77

"Stirring Times on the Ohio Border," *The New York Times*, New York, NY, Sunday, July 21, 1861. Online article: https://www.nytimes.com/1861/07/21/archives/stirring-times-on-the-ohio-border.html

"The Woman's Relief Corps, The 22nd National Convention a Dream of Delight—Boston's Hospitality Overpowering—Election of National Officers," *The National Tribune*, Washington, D.C., Thursday, August 25, 1904. Library of Congress online article: https://chroniclingamerica.loc.gov/data/batches/dlc_abe_ver01/data/sn82016187/100493962/1910071401/0343.pdf

Other Online Articles

"Camp Carrington." (2020) In Ohio Civil War Central, Retrieved May 19, 2020, from Ohio Civil War Central. Online article: http://www.www.ohiocivilwarcentral.com/entry.php?rec=319

"Roles to maintain the armies of the Civil War," American Battlefield Trust. Online article: https://www.battlefields.org/learn/articles/military-staff

"African American West Virginians in the Civil War: The 45th USCT," The Carter Woodson Project, Marshall University, Huntington, WV. Online article: https://www.marshall.edu/woodson-dev/african-american-west-virginians-in-the-civil-war-the-45th-usct/

Mitchell, Silas Weir, *The Medical Department in the Civil War*, reprinted from *The Journal of the American Medical Association*, May 9, 1914, Vol. LXII, pp. 1445-1450. Chicago, IL: American Medical Association, 1914. Online article: https://www.ncbi.nlm.nih.gov/pmc/articles/PMC4790547/

Websites

Gallia County Genealogical Society, OGS Chapter, Inc.: http://www.galliagenealogy.org/index.html

Civil War Veterans, Gallia Genealogical Society: http://www.galliagenealogy.org/civil%20war/CWPhotosIII/index6.htm

Sons of Union Veterans of the Civil War, National Headquarters: http://www.suvcw.org/?page_id=167

National Association of Army Nurses of the Civil War, The American History & Genealogy Project: http://www.ahgp.org/women/national_association_of_army_nurses_civil_war.html

Old Ohio Schools: http://www.oldohioschools.com/gallia_county.htm

Index

This index includes entries from pages 1 through 94 of the book. You may check the appendices separately for names of surgeons, staff, nurses, and soldiers.

NOTES

Introduction

1   Lenette S. Taylor, *'The Supply for Tomorrow Must Not Fail': The Civil War of Captain Simon Perkins Jr., a Union Quartermaster* (Kent & London: The Kent State University Press, 2004), 178.

Chapter One

2   "Miss Hannah U. Maxon Dead: Prominent and Good Woman Passes Away After Long Illness," *Gallipolis Daily Tribune*, May 27, 1910, accessed December 3, 2019. http://bossardlibrary.advantage-preservation.com/viewer/?k=hannah%20maxon&i=f&by=1910&bdd=1910&d=01011910-07311910&m=between&ord=k1&fn=gallipolis_daily_tribune_usa_ohio_gallipolis_19100527_english_4&df=1&dt=10

3   "News of the River," *Gallipolis Daily Tribune*, March 16, 1910, accessed December 3, 2019. http://bossardlibrary.advantage-preservation.com/viewer/?k=william%20phillips&i=f&by=1910&bdd=1910&d=03011910-03311910&m=between&ord=k1&fn=gallipolis_daily_tribune_usa_ohio_gallipolis_19100316_english_3&df=1&dt=1

4   Olivia Odelot, "Papers for Young Schoolmistresses No. II: A Peep at the Reality," *Ohio Educational Monthly and the National Teacher: A Journal of School and Home Education, Old Series, Volume IX, New Series, Volume I,* 1860. 108. Hathitrust Digital Library.

5   *Who's Who in New England, Volume 2* (Chicago: A.N. Marquis & Company, 1916). 1030. https://books.google.com/books?id=RmUTAAAAYAAJ&pg=PA1#v=onepage&q=Lincoln%20R.%20Stone&f=false

6   "Civil War Service Records, Union Records," digital images, Fold3 (http://www.fold3.com: accessed 4 February 2020), 2nd Massachusetts Infantry, pg. 3, headed "Field and Staff Muster-in Roll, entry for Lincoln R. Stone.

7   *The Medical and Surgical History of the War of the Rebellion, Volume I,* (Washington, D.C.: General Printing Office, 1870). https://collections.nlm.nih.gov/bookviewer?PID=nlm:nlmuid-14121350RX1-mvpart

8   Rev. W.W. Lyle, A.M., *Lights and Shadows of Army Life: Or, Pen Pictures from the Battlefield, the Camp and the Hospital* (Cincinnati: R.W. Carroll & Co, 1865). 53. https://books.google.com/books?id=WwdIAQAAMAAJ&pg=P

A392&lpg=PA392&dq=%22J+F+Gabriel%22+surgeon+11th+OVI&source=bl
&ots=tj1NLwXzVa&sig=xp333SxW1Z_zSwN_7zgTOYZP6rU&hl=en&sa=X&ve
d=0ahUKEwiFyajs2IzaAhXM3VMKHaojAQQQ6AEIKTAA#v=onepage&q=Prin
ceton&f=false Hathitrust Digital Library.

9   Ibid., p. 60.

10 *Gallipolis Journal*, January 23, 1862. Accessed January 24, 2020. https://
www.newspapers.com/image/70822705

11 Paul Locher, "Robison was part of several firsts at start of Civil War,"
The Daily Record, Wooster, Ohio, May 14, 2008, accessed June
11, 2020. https://www.the-daily-record.com/news/20080514/
robison-was-part-of-several-firsts-at-start-of-civil-war

12 "James Edward Hanger's Story," Hanger, Inc. website, accessed June 11,
2020. http://www.hanger.com/history/Pages/The-J.E.-Hanger-Story.aspx

13 *Gallipolis Journal*, January 23, 1862, accessed January 24, 2020. https://
www.newspapers.com/image/70822690/?terms=Gabriel&match=1 ()

14 Theodore Wilder, *The History of Company C., Seventh Regiment, O.V.I.,*
(Oberlin: J.B.T. Marsh, 1866). 11. https://books.google.com/books?id=Hp
ZBAAAAYAAJ&q=June+26#v=snippet&q=June%2026&f=false

15 J.F. Harmon and E.F. Grabill, *The Ohio Seventh*, Weston, Virginia (West
Virginia), Vol. 1, No. 1, July 4, 1861.

16 "An Act Respecting Alien Enemies," Congress of the Confederate States of
America, reprinted in *The Richmond Times Dispatch*, August 9, 1861. The
Daily Dispatch digital.http://www.perseus.tufts.edu/hopper/text?doc=Per
seus%3Atext%3A2006.05.0240%3Aarticle%3D12

17 Leroy Warren, copy of *Diary Written During the Civil War*, entry dated
August 27, 1861. Oberlin Heritage Center, Oberlin, Ohio, accessed July 13,
2017.

18 Edgar M. Condit, "An Episode of the Battle of Cross Lanes," *Itinerary of the
Seventh Ohio Volunteer Infantry, 1861-1864,* (New York and Washington:
The Neale Publishing Company, 1907). 347. https://books.google.com/boo
ks?id=tBJCAAAAIAAJ&pg=PA347&lpg=PA347&dq=an+episode+of+the+bat
tle+of+cross+lanes&source=bl&ots=26_R8iloXj&sig=_pkWRzfi4KiD1YWuQf
pp1Y58gSE&hl=en&ei=zaLXTuHVA6HI0AG-xIyMDg&sa=X&oi=book_result
&ct=result&resnum=5&ved=0CDsQ6AEwBA#v=onepage&q&f=true Google
Books.

19   William D. Shepherd, *Itinerary, 92.* https://www.google.com/books/edition/Itinerary_of_the_Seventh_Ohio_Volunteer/tBJCAAAAIAAJ?hl=en&gbpv=1&bsq=Tyler%20Creighton%20Salter%20Brown Google Books.

Chapter Two

20   "Field Hospitals," *New-York Tribune*, September 30, 1864, accessed May 23, 2020. https://www.newspapers.com/clip/47199729/new-york-tribune/ . Newspapers.com.

21   George A. Otis, "Hip-Joint Amputations in the War of the Rebellion," A *Report on Amputations at the Hip-Joint in Military Surgery* (Washington, D.C.: Government Printing Office, 1867). 20. https://books.google.com/books?id=Uz96thwrRBYC&pg=PA20&lpg=PA20&dq=%22Jonas+F.+Gabriel%22OR%22Jonas+Frank+Gabriel%22OR%22J.+Frank+Gabriel%22&source=bl&ots=kuuUnB83s1&sig=ACfU3U0Cu0-sA_eiEOUKX5a32WNQngJu3Q&hl=en&sa=X&ved=2ahUKEwidza_Kp9nnAhVAgXIEHXf8At0Q6AEwAnoECAcQAQ#v=onepage&q=%22Jonas%20F.%20Gabriel%22OR%22Jonas%20Frank%20Gabriel%22OR%22J.%20Frank%20Gabriel%22&f=false Google Books.

22   "Tribute to the memory of Wm. Honeywell, of Co. B, 21st Reg., who died in the Hospital at Gallipolis, June 27th, 1861," *Gallipolis Journal*, June 27, 1861, accessed January 23, 2020. https://www.newspapers.com/image/70832739 Newspapers.com.

23   "Letter From a Sick Soldier," *Gallipolis Journal*, August 8, 1861, accessed June 6, 2020. https://www.newspapers.com/image/50593382# Newspapers.com.

24   U.S. Congress, Report to accompany bill H.R. 3911, Committee on Invalid Pensions, 50th Cong., July 30, 1888.

25   1850 U.S. Census, Licking County, Ohio, population schedule. Sharon Village, Gallipolis Township, p.403, dwelling 29, family 29. Francis and Mary P. Salter; digital image, Ancestry.com, accessed February 6, 2020,

https://www.ancestry.com/imageviewer/collections/7667/images/4284144_00287?treeid=&personid=&hintid=&usePUB=true&_phsrc=OcA5076&_phstart=successSource&usePUBJs=true&_ga=2.96354780.1762647549.1591815002-407736261.1507342369&pId=41774742&backurl=https%3A%2F%2Fsearch.ancestry.com%2Fcgi-bin%2Fsse.dll%3Findiv%3D1%26dbid%3D7667%26h%3D41774742%26tid%3D%26pid%3D%26usePUB%3Dtrue%26_phsrc%3DOcA5076%26_phstart%3DsuccessSource Ancestry.com.

26   Dr. Chancey D. Griswold, Inspection Report, *Documents of the U.S. Sanitary Commission, Vol. I, Numbers 1 to 60.* (New York, 1866). 9. https://books.google.com/books?id=FG8JVKi_p0kC&pg=RA2-PA9&lpg=RA2-PA9&dq=%22Dr.+T.F.+Gabriel%22+Gallipolis&source=bl&ots=yzJiTC27xc&sig=K4m1F9hFx1vzgbwmkp1MagnwkQI&hl=en&sa=X&ved=2ahUKEwjGmtTlpLXaAhXFoFMKHXtUCJsQ6AEwAHoECAAQKg#v=onepage&q=%22Dr.%20T.F.%20Gabriel%22%20Gallipolis&f=false Google Books.

Chapter Three

27   "Stirring Times on the Ohio Border," *The New York Times*, July 21, 1861. Accessed June 11, 2020. https://timesmachine.nytimes.com/timesmachine/1861/07/21/78662309.html?pageNumber=3 New York Times Machine.

28   *Gallipolis Journal*, October 17, 1861. Accessed March 20, 2020. https://www.newspapers.com/image/64246722/?terms=camp%20fever&match=1

29   *Gallipolis Journal*, November 6, 1862. Accessed June 11, 2020. https://www.newspapers.com/image/70825960/?terms=Kline%20House&match=1#) Newspapers.com.

30   *Gallipolis Journal*, January 23, 1862. Accessed January 24, 2020. https://www.newspapers.com/image/70822705 Newspapers.com.

31   United States Veterans Administration Master Index, Hannah U. Maxon, Nurse, Medical Department, US Volunteers Case 2485596. Accessed April 25, 2020. https://www.familysearch.org/ark:/61903/3:1:3Q9M-CS1Y-KHG9-8?cc=2968245&personaUrl=%2Fark%3A%2F61903%2F1%3A1%3AWMJY-4JZM. FamilySearch.org.

32   United States Army, War Department, Adjutant-General's Office, *The Army Surgeon's Manual*, p. 28 (New York: Balliere Brothers, 1864). https://collections.nlm.nih.gov/bookviewer?PID=nlm:nlmuid-62510300R-bk#page/26/mode/2up/search/Dix U.S. National Library of Medicine Digital Collections.

33   *Roster and Proceedings of the Annual Encampment of the Department of Ohio, Grand Army of the Republic, Bellefontaine, Ohio, May 7th, 8th and 9th, 1901*, (Cincinnati, Ohio: The Elm Street Printing Works, 1901). 109. Accessed April 11, 2020. https://books.google.com/books?id=FGJv-SEGdREC&pg=PA92&lpg=PA92&dq=Grand+Army+of+the+Republic+1901+Bellefontaine+Ohio&source=bl&ots=NbG6abM9v9&sig=ACfU3U2lU4ktNtLuJhZSemiIOzgKbGRKmA&hl=en&sa=X&ved=2ahUKEwiT5JGtt_zpAhXaknIEHUNGB0cQ6AEwAHoECAoQAQ#v=onepage&q=Maxon&f=false Google Books.

34   Obituary, Hannah U. Maxon, *Gallipolis Daily Tribune*, reprinted April 9, 1992. Accessed May 5, 2020. http://bossardlibrary.advantage-preservation.com/viewer/?k=hannah%20maxon&i=f&by=1992&bdd=1990&d=01011992-12311992&m=between&ord=k1&fn=gallipolis_daily_tribune_usa_ohio_gallipolis_19920409_english_10&df=1&dt=2 Bossard Library Digital Newspaper Archive.

35   John Lustrea, "Women Nurses in the Civil War," Facebook Live event, National Museum of Civil War Medicine, April 2020. https://www.facebook.com/CivilWarMed/videos/212975689766789/

36   *In honor of the National Association of Civil War Army Nurses*, "Miss Hannah Utla Maxon" (Atlantic City, New Jersey: Citizens Executive Committee, 1910). https://archive.org/details/inhonorofnationa00nati/page/n15/mode/2up?q=Maxon Internet Archive.

37   *Roll of members, address of national president, and report of officers of the National Convention of the Woman's Relief Corps, Atlantic City, New Jersey, September 21, 22 and 23, 1910*, p. 277 (Boston, Massachusetts: Griffith-Stillings Press, 1910). 277.

      https://babel.hathitrust.org/cgi/pt?id=wu.89062150966&view=1up&seq=301&q1=Maxon Hathitrust Digital Library.

Chapter Four

38   *Gallipolis Journal*, May 8, 1862. Accessed June 12, 2020. https://www.newspapers.com/image/70823676# Newspapers.com.

39   "Improvements in Hospital Design," Civil War Rx, http://civilwarrx.blogspot.com/2015/08/improvements-in-hospital-design.html

40   *The Medical and Surgical History of the War of the Rebellion (1861-1865), Volume 1, Part 3* (Washington, D.C.: Government Printing Office, 1888). 908. https://collections.nlm.nih.gov/bookviewer?PID=nlm:nlmuid-14121350RX3-mvpart#page/1008/mode/2up/search/pavilion U.S. National Library of Medicine Digital Collections.

41   Florence Nightingale, "Sanitary Conditions of Hospitals," *Notes on Hospitals*, Third Edition, p. 16 (London: Longman, Green, Longman, Roberts, and Green, 1863) 17. https://archive.org/details/notesonhospital01nighgoog/page/n6/mode/2up?q=vapour Internet Archive.

42   *Medical and Surgical History*, 908.

43   Ibid.

44   "To Our Correspondents," *Gallipolis Journal*, May 22, 1862. Accessed June 12, 2020. https://www.newspapers.com/image/70823853# Newspapers. com.

45   Joseph R. Lunbeck papers, digital images, Virginia Military Institute Digital Collections. http://digitalcollections.vmi.edu/digital/collection/p15821coll11/id/3426, accessed March 30, 2020.

46   J.O. Breeden, "The Winchester Accord: The Confederacy and the Humane Treatment of Captive Medical Officers," *Military Medicine*, November 1993. 689-92. https://pubmed.ncbi.nlm.nih.gov/8284050/ PubMed.gov.

Chapter Five

47   Jane E. Schultz, *Women at the Front: Hospital Workers in Civil War America.* (Chapel Hill, NC: The University of North Carolina Press, 2005). 131. https://www.google.com/books/edition/Women_at_the_Front/PVc85-x1p3QC?hl=en&gbpv=0

48   *Gallipolis Journal*, May 29 1862. Accessed June 12, 2020. https://www.newspapers.com/image/70823943/?terms=Moulton&match=1# Newspapers.com.

49   Katherine Dannehl, "Dr. Lincoln R. Stone, Civil War Surgeon," *The Beehive* blog, August 4, 2017. http://www.masshist.org/beehiveblog/2017/08/dr-lincoln-r-stone-civil-war-surgeon/

50   U.S. Army General Hospital Gallipolis buildings and grounds, drawings, digital images, Massachusetts Historical Society website, http://www.masshist.org/beehiveblog/2017/08/dr-lincoln-r-stone-civil-war-surgeon/

51   Charles Tripler and George Blackman, *Handbook for the Military Surgeon* (Cincinatti, Ohio: Robert Clarke & Co, Publishers, 1861) 6. https://books.google.com/books?id=S3Y-AAAAIAAJ&printsec=frontcover&source=gbs_ge_summary_r&cad=0#v=onepage&q&f=false Google Books.

52   Joseph Woodward, *The Hospital Steward's Manual* (Philadelphia: J.B. Lippincott & Co., 1862). 112-116. https://archive.org/details/hospital-stewards00unse/ Internet Archive.

53   William Grace, *The Army Surgeon's Manual for the Use of Medical Officers, Cadets, Chaplains, and Hospital Stewards, Second Edition.* (New York: Balliere Brothers, 1865) https://collections.nlm.nih.gov/bookviewer?PID=nlm:nlmuid-62510300R-bk#page/1/mode/1up U.S. National Library of Medicine Digital Collections.

54   Ibid.

55   Woodward, *The Hospital Steward's Manual*, 25-27.

56   Ibid,.47-50.

57   A Committee of Hospital Physicians of the City of New York, *Manual of Directions Prepared for the Use of Nurses in the Army Hospitals*, published by the Women's Central Association of Relief to the Army (New York: Baker & Goodwin, Printers, 1861).

58   Ibid.

59   Charles Dinneford, *A family medicine directory, Fourth Edition*, (London: Simpkin, Marshall, And Co.; Dinneford and Co., 1854). 84. https://books. google.com/books?id=0RMDAAAAQAAJ&printsec=frontcover&source=gbs_ge_summary_r&cad=0#v=onepage&q&f=false Google Books.

60   *Gallipolis Journal*, August 21, 1862. Accessed June 12, 2020. https:// www.newspapers.com/image/70824998/?terms=Governor%20David%20Tod%20vegetables&match=1# Newspapers.com.

61   *Gallipolis Journal*, August 7, 1862. Accessed June 12, 2020. https://www.newspapers.com/image/70824851/ Newspapers.com.

62   Annie Wittenmyer, *Under the Guns: A Woman's Reminiscences of the Civil War* (Boston, Massachusetts: E.B. Stillings & Co., Publishers, 1895). 79. https://books.google.com/books?id=3dI_AQAAMAAJ&printsec=frontcover&source=gbs_ge_summary_r&cad=0#v=onepage&q&f=false Google Books.

63   Ibid.

64   Ibid, p. 80.

65   Ibid, p. 82.

Chapter Six

66   *Gallipolis Journal*, July 3, 1862. Accessed on February 24, 2020.

67   Terry Lowry, *22nd Virginia Infantry, The Virginia Regimental History Series* (Lynchburg, Virginia: H.E. Howard, Inc., 1988), Second Edition, 2. "George S. Patton," bio, Shenandoah Valley Battlefields National Historic District website. Accessed June 13, 2020 https://www.shenandoahatwar.org/history/george-s-patton/

68   William Bahlmann and Rob Abbot, Ed., *Down in the Ranks or Bread and Blankets: An account of his military service in the Confederate Armed Forces, 1861 to 1865* (self-pub) 48-49.

69   Cushing, Mrs. M.M., letter, reprinted in The Gallia County Glade, Vol. 33, No. 4, Winter 2008.

70 "Traitors Will Take Notice," *Gallipolis Journal*, August 8, 1862. Accessed on Sept. 6, 2019.
https://www.newspapers.com/image/70824901/?terms=%22James%2BR.%2BBell%22 Newspapers.com.

71 "Tell Us the Reason Why," *Gallipolis Journal*, August 28, 1862. Acessed August 27, 2019. https://www.newspapers.com/image/70825084 Newspapers.com.

72 *Gallipolis Journal*, August 21, 1862. Accessed June 13, 2020.https://www.newspapers.com/image/70824998/?terms=Gallipolis,%20Ohio&match=1# Newspapers.com.

73 "The Management of the Hospital at Gallipolis," *Gallipolis Journal*, August 28, 1862. Accessed August 27, 2019. https://www.newspapers.com/image/70825143/?terms=Bell&match=1 Newspapers.com.

74 *Gallipolis Journal*, September 18, 1862. Accessed January 27, 2020.

75 "Civil War Service Records, Union Records," digital images, Fold3(https://www.fold3.com/image/266925201, accessed December 19, 2019), Company H, Ninth West Virginia Infantry, pg. 2, headed "Company Descriptive Book, entry for Joseph Russell Wheeler.

76 "Compiled Service Records of Volunteer Union Soldiers Who Served in Organizations from the State of West Virginia," digital images, Fold3 (https://www.fold3.com/image/21/266925226, accessed December 19, 2019), pg. 13, headed "Certificate of Disability for Discharge," entry for Joseph Russell Wheeler.

77 *The Wenatchee Daily World* (Washington State), February 14, 1916. Accessed March 20, 2020. https://www.ancestry.com/mediaui-viewer/collection/1030/tree/108581749/person/390069853880/media/0b9b4551-e7aa-47ff-a589-7341863b204b?_phsrc=OcA5102&usePUBJs=true Ancestry.com.

78 Guides, Civil War, "Restored Government," Library of Virginia website. Accessed June 22, 2020. https://www.lva.virginia.gov/public/guides/Civil-War/Restored-Government.htm#:~:text=The%20convention%20voted%20to%20defy,recognized%20by%20President%20Abraham%20Lincoln.

79 "Gunshot Contusions of the Cranial Bones, Wounds and Injuries of the Head," *The Medical and Surgical History of the War of the Rebellion, Volume 2, Part 1*, (Washington, D.C.: Government Printing Office, 1870). 119. https://collections.nlm.nih.gov/

bookviewer?PID=nlm:nlmuid-14121350RX4-mvpart#page/282/mode/2up/ search/Beel U.S. National Library of Medicine Digital Collections.

80   "Register of Confederates and Civilians Who Died in the North, 1861-1865,"digital images FamilySearch (https://www.familysearch.org/ ark:/61903/3:1:3QS7-89Z5-FBCL?i=459&cc=2250054&personaUrl=%2Fa rk%3A%2F61903%2F1%3A1%3AQV1W-BSBT, accessed March 21, 2020). pg. 449, headed "List of Confederate soldiers who, while prisoners of war, died at Gallipolis, Ohio., entry for Robert J. Thrasher."

81   "Gallia County News During the War," *Gallipolis Journal*, transcription, October 9, 1862. Accessed January 21, 2020. http://www.galliageneal-ogy.org/Civil%20War/warnews.htm . Gallia County Genealogical Society website.

82   "From Western Virginia," reprint from *The Cincinnati Commercial* in The Weekly Register (Point Pleasant, Virginia). Accessed December 3, 2019. https://www.newspapers.com/image/171157498# Newspapers.com.

83   "News Items from the *Gallipolis Journal* During the Civil War Years," tran-scription, November 27, 1862. Accessed June 14, 2020. http://www.gal-liagenealogy.org/History/cwyears.htm#top Gallia County Genealogical Society website.

84   *Gallipolis Journal*, January 1, 1863. Accessed September 6, 2019. https:// www.newspapers.com/image/70853237 Newspapers.com.

Chapter Eight

85   William Waddell Mills, "Letter from the Eighteenth Ohio," *Gallipolis Journal*, January 22, 1863
      Accessed April 7, 2020 https://www.newspapers.com/image/70853519 Newspapers.com.

86   *Gallipolis Journal*, February 12, 1863. Accessed January 26, 2020. https:// www.newspapers.com/image/70853866 Newspapers.com.

87   *Gallipolis Journal*, June 11, 1863. Accessed September 6, 2019. https:// www.newspapers.com/image/70855040 Newspapers.com.

88   Ibid.

89   "Civil War Service Records, Union Records," digital images, Fold3 (https:// www.fold3.com/image/265754470 accessed April 2, 2020). Company A, Fourth West Virginia Infantry, pg. 2, headed "Record and Pension Office, War Department, Washington, Nov. 23, 1889, entry for James Driver."

90   *Gallipolis Journal*, June 11, 1863. Accessed December 3, 2019. https://
      www.newspapers.com/image/70855040 Newspapers.com.

91   *Gallipolis Journal*, June 18, 1863. Accessed January 22, 2020. https://
      www.newspapers.com/image/70855123 Newspapers.com.

92   "War Meeting!" *Gallipolis Journal*, April 16, 1863. Accessed June 16, 2020.
      https://www.newspapers.com/image/70854531/?terms=rebel%2Barms#

93   "Morgan's Raid," Ohio History Central. Accessed June 16, 2020. https://
      ohiohistorycentral.org/w/Morgan%27s_Raid

94   *Gallipolis Journal*, June 25, 1863. Accessed June 16, 2020. https://www.
      newspapers.com/image/50632505/?terms=colored&match=1 Newspapers.
      com.

95   DeNeen L. Brown, "Frederick Douglass needed to see Lincoln. Would the
      president meet with a former slave?" *The Washington Post*, February 14,
      2018. Accessed December 3, 2019 https://www.washingtonpost.com/
      news/retropolis/wp/2018/02/14/frederick-douglass-needed-to-see-lin-
      coln-would-the-president-meet-with-a-former-slave/

96   Douglas R. Edgerton, *Thunder at the Gates: The Black Civil War Regiments
      That Redeemed America.* (Philadelphia, Pennsylvania: Basic Books).42.
      https://books.google.com/books?id=cinXCwAAQBAJ&pg=PT96&lpg=PT
      96&dq=%E2%80%9CI+really+think+they+showed+themselves+very+bra
      ve,+true+soldiers+in+both+of+the+engagements+they+have+been+in.%
      E2%80%9D&source=bl&ots=-R88AKaL5C&sig=ACfU3U2BM9J3KpwQG
      Ysa_TjXwVilReW_TA&hl=en&sa=X&ved=2ahUKEwifhZCx0YbqAhXVl3IEH
      dh9CrcQ6AEwAHoECAEQAQ#v=onepage&q=%E2%80%9CI%20really%20
      think%20they%20showed%20themselves%20very%20brave%2C%20
      true%20soldiers%20in%20both%20of%20the%20engagements%20they%20
      have%20been%20in.%E2%80%9D&f=false Google Books.

97   Marriage announcement, J.R. Lunbeck and Agnes Truslow,
      Gallipolis Journal, October 5, 1863. Accessed December 31, 2019)
      https://www.newspapers.com/search/beta/#query=Lunbeck&s_
      place=Gallipolis%2C+OH&dr_year=1863-1863 Newspapers.com.

Chapter Nine

98   Rev. W.W. Lyle, A.M., *Lights and Shadows of Army Life: Or, Pen Pictures
      from the Battlefield, the Camp and the Hospital* (Cincinnati: R.W. Carroll &
      Co, 1865). 64. https://books.google.com/books?id=WwdIAQAAMAAJ&pg=P
      A392&lpg=PA392&dq=%22J+F+Gabriel%22+surgeon+11th+OVI&source=bl
      &ots=tj1NLwXzVa&sig=xp333SxW1Z_zSwN_7zgTOYZP6rU&hl=en&sa=X&ve

d=0ahUKEwiFyajs2IzaAhXM3VMKHaojAQQQ6AEIKTAA#v=onepage&q=Prin
ceton&f=false Hathitrust Digital Library.

99   *Thirty-Eighth Annual Report of The American Tract Society, presented at New York, May 13, 1863.* (New York: American Tract Society). https://
books.google.com/books?id=IJE_AQAAMAAJ&pg=PA46&lpg=PA46&
dq=%22Rev.+Mr.+Blake%22+%22American+Tract+Society%22+Bost
on+1863&source=bl&ots=avvIGtgrPs&sig=ACfU3U3PhNO 0d0WssZA
M5YCxALIbIDkUXw&hl=en&sa=X&ved=2ahUKEwiOj6v104bqAhX5on
EHa-NClsQ6AEwCnoECAkQAQ#v=onepage&q=%22Rev.%20Mr.%20
Blake%22%20%22American%20Tract%20Society%22%20Boston%20
1863&f=false Google Books.

100 General Orders No. 55, War Department, Adjutant-General's Office, Washington, May 24, 1862. *The Army Surgeon's Manual (New York: Balliere Brothers, 1864). 44.* https://collections.nlm.nih.gov/
bookviewer?PID=nlm:nlmuid-62510300R-bk#page/42/mode/1up/
search/44 U.S. National Library of Medicine Digital Collections.

101 "The Pay of Chaplains," *Urbana Union, February 24, 1864. Accessed March 31, 2020.* https://www.newspapers.com/image/143613823/?terms=chapl
ain&match=1 Newspapers.com.

102 *Gallipolis Journal, August 21, 1862. Accessed December 11, 2019.* https://
www.newspapers.com/image/70824998/?terms=French&match=1#
Newspapers.com.

103 *Diary and Letters of Rutherford Birchard Hayes, Nineteenth President of the United States, Volume 2, 1861-1865, (Columbus, Ohio: The F.J. Heer Printing Company). 268-269.* https://archive.org/details/
DiaryAndLettersOfRutherfordBirchardHayesNineteenthPresidentOfThe_
657/ page/n291/mode/2up?q=French Internet Archive.

104 John P. Deeben, "Faith on the Firing Line: Army Chaplains in the Civil War," *Prologue Magazine, Spring 2016. Accessed June 16, 2020.* https://
www.archives.gov/publications/prologue/2016/spring/chaplains.html
National Archives website.

105 Ibid.

106 *Gallipolis Journal, March 24, 1864. Accessed September 23, 2019.* https://
www.newspapers.com/image/70859500/?terms=abandoned%20
women&match=1 Newspapers.com.

107 Ibid.

108 "Civil War Service Records, Union Records," digital images, Fold3 (https://www.fold3.com/image/267386263, accessed January 14, 2020), pg. 5, headed "Company Muster Roll Card, Company D, 9th Regiment Virginia Infantry," May and June, 1864, entry for William Hickman.

109 *Memorial R.G.S. [Robert Gould Shaw], (Cambridge, Massachusetts: University Press, 1864). 52.* https://archive.org/details/memorialrgsrober-00cambuoft/page/28/mode/2up?q=Lincoln+R.+Stone Internet Archive.

110 E.D. Townsend, General Orders No. 23, War Department, Adjutant General's Office, Washington, January 16, 1864. https://collections.nlm.nih.gov/bookviewer?PID=nlm:nlmuid-101533508-bk#page/1/mode/1up U.S. National Library of Medicine Digital Collections.

111 Henry Rittenhouse, letter from U.S. Army Medical Purveyor's Office, Cincinnati, Ohio, August 6, 1864. Found in collection of letters received by Surgeon Lincoln R. Stone, 1864. Accessed December 2019. National Archives and Records Administration.

112 *The American Medical Times, Vol. VIII, January to June, 1864 (New York: Bailliere Brothers, 1864) p. 84.* https://books.google.com/books?id=G4xMAQAAMAAJ&pg=PA84&lpg=PA84&dq=%22Surgeon+Lincoln+R.+Stone%22+Gallipolis&source=bl&ots=C4mK6Wd_sD&sig=ACfU3U3eTDNU35B2DFM7e-mqIJ7XY3-fCw&hl=en&sa=X&ved=2ahUKEwjZwKXH6YbqAhVRhXIEHSwmBnQQ6AEwBHoECAYQAQ#v=onepage&q=%22Surgeon%20Lincoln%20R.%20Stone%22%20Gallipolis&f=false Google Books.

113 "Marriages Registered in the City of Boston, 1840-1915, LIncoln R. Stone, spouse Harriet Hodges, Ancestry.com (https://www.ancestry.com/imageviewer/collections/2511/images/41262_b139489-00194?treeid=&personid=&rc=&usePUB=true&_phsrc=OcA5106&_phstart=successSource&pId=1050794840&backurl=https%3A%2F%2Fwww.ancestry.com%2Fsearch%2Fcategories%2F34%2F%3Fname%3DLincoln%2BR._Stone%26event%3D_Salem-Massachusetts%26birth%3D1825%26gender%3Dm%26keyword%3DSurgeon%2C%2Bphysician%26location%3D2%26marriage%3D1864_salem-essex-massachusetts-usa_4397%26name_x%3D_1%26priority%3Dusa%26race%3Dwhite%26residence%3D_newton-middlesex-massachusetts-usa_4542%26spouse%3DHarriet_Hodges%26_ga%3D2.216515486.968495010.1592328535-407736261.1507342369%26_phtarg%3DOcA5105%26queryId%3Db995e851c23435882d569bed951ece92%26successSource%3DSearch , pg. 1744, accessed June 16, 2020)

114 John C. Myers, *A daily journal of the 192d Regiment Pennsylvania Volunteers, commanded by Col. William B. Thomas, in the service of the*

United States for one hundred days (Philadelphia, Pennsylvania: Crissy & Markley). , 90-91. Retrieved from https://archive.org/details/daily-journalof1900myer/page/90/mode/2up Internet Archive.

115 *Gallipolis Journal, June 16, 1864. Accessed September 23, 2019.* https://www.newspapers.com/image/70860382 Newspapers.com.

116 Civil War papers, Joseph Lunbeck, 1861-1864, accessed March 31, 2020. http://digitalcollections.vmi.edu/digital/collection/p15821coll11/id/3424/rec/1) Virginia Military Institute Archives Digital Collections.

117 Frankfort, "Gen. Crook's Brilliant Achievements in Southwestern Virginia," *The Wheeling Daily Intelligencer, May 27, 1864. Accessed June 16, 2020.* https://www.newspapers.com/image/171194522/?terms=Cloyd%27s%2B Mountain# Newspapers.com.

118 G.M. Kellogg, "Extract from a Report on the Wounded at the Engagements at Cloyd's Mountain and New River Bridge, *The Medical and Surgical History of the War of the Rebellion, 1861-1865 (Washington: Government Printing Office, 1870) 227.* https://books.google.com/books?id=ZAVTAAAAcAAJ&pg=RA3-PA227&lpg=RA3-PA227&dq=%E2%80%9CI+took+one+hundred+and+ninety-two+wounded+to+hospital+at+Gallipolis,+Ohio&source=bl&ots=4sk2TwALUD&sig=ACfU3U1ZiW_KF236lV-ecy_3J8brly55Nw&hl=en&sa=X&ved=2ahUKEwid3q2E-IbqAhXbmnIEHSuXBKEQ6AEwAHoECAUQAQ#v=onepage&q=%E2%80%9CI%20took%20one%20hundred%20and%20ninety-two%20wounded%20to%20hospital%20at%20Gallipolis%2C%20Ohio&f=false Google Books.

119 "Civil War Records, Union Records," digital images, Fold3 (https://www.fold3.com/image/265725580, accessed January 6, 2020), pg.8, headed "Certificate of Disability for Discharge," Company D, 1st West Virginia Veteran Infantry, entry for Zachariah Nicely.

120 Surgeon L.R. Stone, Letter to Editor, *Gallipolis Journal, July 14, 1864. Accessed June 16, 2020*

https://www.newspapers.com/image/70860647/?terms=Gallipolis,%20Ohio&match=1# Newspapers.com.

121 *Gallipolis Journal, July 7, 1864. Accessed September 6, 2019.*

https://www.newspapers.com/image/?clipping_id=35670500&fcfToken=eyJhbGciOiJIUzI1NiIsInR5cCI6IkpXVCJ9.eyJmcmVlLXZpZXctaWQiOjc-wODYwNTUyLCJpYXQiOjE1OTIzMzI0NzUsImV4cCI6MTU5MjQxODg3NX0.43xyjmqqEHCwD4zj_7UKqlxf_eAxCtqBSyK43MikHzc Newspapers.com.

122 Ibid.

123   Edward Hanrahan, letter to Assistant Adjutant General Samuel Breck. Found in collection of letters received by Surgeon Lincoln R. Stone, 1864. Accessed December 2019. National Archives and Records Administration.

124   Correspondence and orders from the U.S. Army General Hospital, Gallipolis, Ohio, 1864-1865. Box 1 of 1, Folder 1, Call letter MSC24. Accessed August 2017. Found at National Institutes of Health, National Library of Medicine Historical Medical Collection.

125   Charles Tripler, letter to Surgeon L.R. Stone. Found in collection of letters received by Surgeon Lincoln R. Stone, 1864. Accessed December 2019. National Archives and Records Administration.

126   "Letters Received by the Adjutant General, Civil War, 1864," pg.2. Max Joseph Keonig letter to C.A. Finley, M.D., Surgeon General, U.S.A., digital images, Fold3.com (https://www.fold3.com/image/299769310 , accessed January 27, 2020).

127   "Letters Received by the Adjutant General, Civil War, 1861," pg. 11. A.J. Johnson, letter written at Camp Jersey, Meridian Hill, NJ, dated Oct. 26, 1861. Retrieved from Fold3.com (https://www.fold3.com/image/299769321 accessed January 27, 2020)

128   *Gallipolis Journal, July 7, 1864. Accessed June 16, 2020.* https://www.newspapers.com/image/?clipping_id=35670500&fcfToken=eyJhbGciOiJIUzI1NiIsInR5cCI6IkpXVCJ9.eyJmcmVlLXZpZXctaWQiOjcwODYwNTUyL-CJpYXQiOjE1OTIzMzl0NzUsImV4cCI6MTU5MjQxODg3NX0.43xyjmqqEHCwD4zj_7UKqlxf_eAxCtqBSyK43MikHzc# Newspapers.com.

129   Ibid.

130   Ibid.

Chapter Ten

131   *Gallipolis Journal*, January 1, 1863. Accessed April 7, 2020.

132   General Order No. 72, 1862, *The War of the Rebellion: A compilation of the Official Records of the Union and Confederate Armies, Series II—Volume V (Washington, D.C.: Government Printing Office, 1899). 260.* https://books.google.com/books?id=L1Be6fh0bUkC&pg=PA260&lpg=PA260&dq=Whenever+sick+men,+paroled+prisoners+or+others,+under+circumstances+entitling+them+to+their+descriptive+lists&source=bl&ots=hyi12aKsd8&sig=ACfU3U1W-B-LLMVDfTJyibygPicB9ZcAOg&hl=en&sa=X&ved=2ahUKEwiS9Ke2-IjqAhU2knIEHcyMAEQQ6AEwB3oECAkQAQ#v=onepage&q=Whenever%20sick%20men%2C%20paroled%20prisoners%20or%20others%2C%20

under%20circumstances%20entitling%20them%20to%20their%20
descriptive%20lists&f=false

133 Ella Lonn, *Desertion During the Civil War (New York and London: The
Century Co.). p. 41. Accessed January 8, 2020.* https://babel.hathitrust.
org/cgi/pt?id=uc1.$b61319&view=1up&seq=57&q1=hospital Hathitrust
Digital Library.

134 "Weekly Report of U.S. Gen. Hospital, Gallipolis, O., *Gallipolis Journal,
February 4, 1864.*

Accessed April 3, 2020.https://www.newspapers.com/image/70858907/?t
erms=hospital&match=1 Newspapers.com.

135 Civil War Service Records, Union Records," digital images, Fold3 (https://
www.fold3.com/image/268601879, accessed April 7, 2020), pg. 18, headed
"Descriptive List of Deserters from the Post of Wheeling, West Virginia,
January 31, 1865, entry for Martin Sowards.

136 Special Order No. 140, Post Head Quarters, Gallipolis, Ohio, June 23,
1864. Found in collection of letters received by Surgeon Lincoln R.
Stone, 1864, accessed December 2019. National Archives and Records
Administration.

137 Special Order no. 163, Post Head Quarters, Gallipolis, O., July 9[th,] 1864.
Found in collection of letters received by Surgeon Lincoln R. Stone, 1864.
Accessed December 2019) National Archives and Records Administration.

138 *Gallipolis Journal*, June 16, 1864. Accessed September 23, 2019)

https://www.newspapers.com/image/70860382/?terms=hospital&ma
tch=1 Newspapers.com.

139 "Civil War Service Records, Union Records," digital images, Fold3 (https://
www.fold3.com/image/268642861 , accessed January 12, 2020), pg.4,
headed "Returns, Company B, 13 Regiment W.Va. Infantry, May and June
1864," entry for Ezekiel H. Wilson.

140 "Civil War Service Records, Union Records," digital images, Fold3 (https://
www.fold3.com/image/267949875 , accessed December 27, 2019),
pg.3, headed "Company Muster-out Roll, Company I, 13 Regiment W.Va.
Infantry, Wheeling, W.Va., June 22, 1865."

Chapter Eleven

141 Circular, J.T. Nagle, M.D., from *Records* of the Association of Acting
Assistant Surgeons of the United States Army (Salem, MA: Salem Press
Pub. and Print. Co.), 1891. Internet Archive archive.org.

142 *Annual Report of the Surgeon General, to the Governor of Ohio, for the Year1864. (Columbus, Ohio: Richard Nevins, State Printer, 1865). 70.* https://archive.org/details/annualreportofsu00ohiorich/page/70/mode/2up?q=Livesay Internet Archive.

143 Mary Gillett, *The Army Medical Department, 1818-1865 (Washington, D.C.: Center of Military History, United States Army, 1987).181.* https://archive.org/details/TheArmyMedicalDepartment18181865/page/n195/mode/2up?q=quacks Internet Archive.

144 George Washington Livesay, Thomas Livesay Lineage Page. Accessed January 21, 2020. http://joepayne.org/geneybeney/livesay/livesay.htm

145 "George W. Livesay," Soldier History, American Civil War Research Database. Accessed November 2019. Bossard Memorial Library, Gallipolis, Ohio.

146 Obituary, Gallia County Historical and Genealogical Society. Accessed via email January 29, 2020.

147 "Riverby House," Ohio Memory Collection, image and description. Accessed June 17, 2020. https://www.ohiomemory.org/digital/collection/p267401coll36/id/18956 Ohio History Connection website.

148 General Orders No. 59, War Department, Adjutant General's Office, Washington, D.C., August 17, 1864. (New York: Balliere Brothers, 1864).30. https://collections.nlm.nih.gov/bookviewer?PID=nlm:nlmuid-62510300R-bk#page/28/mode/1up/search/General+Orders+No.+59 U.S. National Library of Medicine Digital Collections.

Chapter Twelve

149 "Blind Memorandum," August 23, 1864, *Abraham Lincoln Papers*, Manuscript Division, Library of Congress.

150 Michelle Krowl, "Abraham Lincoln's 'Blind Memorandum,' *Library of Congress blog, August 21, 2014. Accessed June 17, 2020.* https://blogs.loc.gov/loc/2014/08/abraham-lincolns-blind-memorandum/#:~:text=Abraham%20Lincoln%2C%20text%20of%20%E2%80%9CBlind,Manuscript%20Division%2C%20Library%20of%20Congress.&text=He%20took%20it%20to%20a,sight%20unseen%2C%20which%20they%20did.

151 Jonathan White, "How Lincoln Won the Soldier Vote," *Disunion blog, November 7, 2014. Accessed June 17, 2020.* https://opinionator.blogs.

nytimes.com/2014/11/07/how-lincoln-won-the-soldier-vote/ *New York Times Opinionator.*

152 Charles Tripler, letter to Surgeon Lincoln R. Stone, Head-Quarters Northern Department, Medical Director's Office, Cincinnati, O., November 2, 1864. Found in collection of letters received by Surgeon Lincoln R. Stone, 1864. Accessed December 2019. National Archives and Records Administration.

153 Samuel Breck, letter to Charles Tripler, from Major General Hooker's office, October 26th, 1864. Found in collection of letters received by Surgeon Lincoln R. Stone, 1864. Accessed December 2019. National Archives and Records Administration.

Chapter Thirteen

154 Muster-out Roll Card, fold3.com.

155 Civil War Records, Union Records," digital images, Fold3 (https://www.fold3.com/image/21/260680957, accessed January 12, 2020), pg. 9, headed "Company Descriptive Book, Company H, 2nd Regiment W.Va. Cavalry," entry for David W. Cherrington.

156 Civil War Records, Union Records," digital images, Fold3 (Company H, 2nd Regiment W.Va. Cavalry, Company Muster-out Roll Card, dated November 29, 1864. Retrieved from Fold3.com (https://www.fold3.com/image/260680951 , accessed January 12, 2020), pg. 3, headed "Company Muster-out Roll, Company H, 2nd West Virginia Cavalry," entry for David W. Cherrington.

157 *General Army Hospital of Gallipolis, Ohio, in Conjunction with Camp Carrington, Correspondence, Orders, Rules and Regulations, 1865-1865. Original source: National Library of Medicine, History of Medicine Division, Bethesda, Maryland. Copy provided to the author by Randall Fulks, Research Librarian, Bossard Memorial Library, Gallipolis, Ohio, November 2019.*

158 Lincoln Stone, letter to Surgeon A.B. Campbell, U.S. Volunteers, Medical Department of West Virginia, written from U.S.A. General Hospital, Gallipolis, Ohio, March 2nd, 1865. Letter found in Folder 2, Call Number MSC24, *U.S. Army General Hospital, Gallipolis, Ohio, Orders and Correspondence, accessed August 2017, National Library of Medicine, History of Medicine Division, Bethesda, Maryland.*

159 Civil War "Widows' Pension, Ohio, Company F., Infantry, Regiment 34," certified May 8, 1869, Fold3 (https://www.fold3.com/image/1/313153215 , accessed January 20, 2020), pg. 49-50, entry for Lucian B. White.

160 Full diet or half diet?" digital image, *Fugitive Leaves blog, accessed December 3, 2019.* https://histmed.collegeofphysicians.org/full-diet-or-half-diet/ The Historical Medical Library of The College of Physicians of Philadelphia website.

161 Ad, *Gallipolis Journal, March 23, 1865. Accessed March 31, 2020.* https://www.newspapers.com/image/70815460 Newspapers.com.

162 "Civil War Service Records, Union Records," digital images, Fold3 (https://www.fold3.com/image/21/260680985, accessed January 12, 2020), pg 37, headed "Medical Director's Office, Northern Department, Cincinnati, Ohio, June 6, 1865," entry for David W. Cherrington.

163 Lincoln R. Stone, M.D., Case 593, "Diarrhea and Dysentery, Morbid Appearances Observed in Fatal Cases,*" The Surgical and Medical History of the War of the Rebellion, Volume 1, Part 2 (Washington, D.C.: Government Printing Office, 1879). 212. Retrieved from* https://collections.nlm.nih.gov/bookviewer?PID=nlm:nlmuid-14121350RX2-mvpart#page/232/mode/2up/search/Lincoln+R.+Stone (accessed December 17, 2019) U.S. National Library of Medicine Digital Collections.

Chapter Fourteen

164 *Gallipolis Journal*, April 13, 1865. Accessed January 22, 2020.

165 "10 Facts: The Petersburg Campaign, June 15, 1864-April 2, 1865," accessed June 18, 2020. https://www.battlefields.org/learn/articles/10-facts-petersburg-campaign *American Battlefield Trust website.*

166 Ulysses S. Grant, letter to General Robert E. Lee, April 9, 1865. *Personal Memoirs of U.S. Grant. 67.*

http://www.perseus.tufts.edu/hopper/text?doc=Perseus%3Atext%3A2001.05.0019%3Achapter%3D67 Perseus Digital Library, Tufts University.

167 U.S. Grant, letter to E.M. Stanton, published in the *Gallipolis Journal, April 13, 1865. Accessed June 18, 2020.* https://www.newspapers.com/image/70815801 Newspapers.com.

168 R.L. Stewart, "The Surrender of Lee," *Gallipolis Journal, April 13, 1865. Accessed June 18, 2020.*

https://www.newspapers.com/image/70815801 Newspapers.com.

169 *Gallipolis Journal, April 13, 1865. Accessed January 22, 2020.* https://
www.newspapers.com/image/70815828 Newspapers.com.

Chapter Fifteen

170 Jacob Wickerham, diary and account book, March 18 to June 24, 1865,
entry dated April 15th, 1865, pg.17. Accessed May 2020. https://media.
library.ohio.edu/digital/collection/p15808coll6/id/4896 Ohio University
Libraries Digital Archival Collections.

171 "Miss Harris' Account of the President's Murder," *Gallipolis Journal, April
20, 1865. Accessed March 14, 2022. https://www.newspapers.com/image/
70815914/?terms=Lincoln&match=1]*

172 *Gallipolis Journal, June 15, 1865. Accessed June 18, 2020.*

https://www.newspapers.com/image/70816479/?terms=Bell&match=1
Newspapers.com.

173 Ibid. Accessed December 3, 2019. https://www.newspapers.com/
image/70816459 Newspapers.com.

174 G.W. Stipp, letter to Lincoln Stone, headed "Medical Inspector's Office,
Cincinnati, Ohio, June 1, 1865." *General Army Hospital of Gallipolis, Ohio,
in Conjunction with Camp Carrington, Correspondence, Orders, Rules and
Regulations, 1865-1865. Original source: National Library of Medicine,
History of Medicine Division, Bethesda, Maryland. Copy provided to the
author by Randall Fulks, Research Librarian, Bossard Memorial Library,
Gallipolis, Ohio, November 2019.*

175 Lincoln R. Stone, M.D. letter to A.N. Dougherty, M.D., U.S. Volunteers,
Medical Director, headed "Department of W.Va., June 9, 1865." *General
Army Hospital of Gallipolis, Ohio, in Conjunction with Camp Carrington,
Correspondence, Orders, Rules and Regulations, 1865-1865. Original
source: National Library of Medicine, History of Medicine Division, Bethesda,
Maryland. Copy provided to the author by Randall Fulks, Research
Librarian, Bossard Memorial Library, Gallipolis, Ohio, November 2019.*

176 A.N. Dougherty, letter to Surgeon Lincoln R. Stone, U.S. Volunteers, June
9, 1865. *General Army Hospital of Gallipolis, Ohio, in Conjunction with
Camp Carrington, Correspondence, Orders, Rules and Regulations, 1865-
1865. Original source: National Library of Medicine, History of Medicine
Division, Bethesda, Maryland. Copy provided to the author by Randall Fulks,
Research Librarian, Bossard Memorial Library, Gallipolis, Ohio, November
2019.*

177 *Gallipolis Journal, June 22, 1865. Accessed April 23, 2020.* https://www.
     newspapers.com/image/70816531 Newspapers.com.

178 *Gallipolis Journal, August 24, 1865. Accessed January 22, 2020.* https://
     www.newspapers.com/image/70817002 Newspapers.com.

179 *Gallipolis Journal, October 26, 1865. Accessed June 18, 2020.* https://www.
     newspapers.com/image/46350746/ Newspapers.com.

Chapter Sixteen

180 Hannah Maxon, speech, Woman's Relief Corps National Convention,
     Journal of the Thirteenth Annual Convention of the Woman's Relief Corps,
     Auxiliary to the Grand Army of the Republic, Louisville, Kentucky, September
     12th, 13th and 14th, 1895 (Boston, Massachusetts: E.B. Stillings & Co, 1895).
     202. https://books.google.com/books?id=HNgSAAAAYAAJ&pg=PA202&lpg
     =PA202&dq=%22Hannah+Maxon%22+nurse&source=bl&ots=LsqmrQa-wv
     &sig=ACfU3U3q6tlaxvwgGXhfCBP1AVKjRJQh2Q&hl=en&sa=X&ved=2ahU
     KEwjLx9HXkqbkAhXlRt8KHU7kCBcQ6AEwDHoECAkQAQ#v=onepage&q&f
     =false Google Books

181 Ad, *Gallipolis Journal, April 17, 1866. Accessed April 27, 2020.*

     https://www.newspapers.com/image/?clipping_id=49689604&fcfToken=e
     yJhbGciOiJIUzI1NiIsInR5cCI6IkpXVCJ9.eyJmcmVlLXZpZXctaWQiOjcwN-
     zg2Nzc5LCJpYXQiOjE1OTI1MDE5OTcsImV4cCI6MTU5MjU4ODM5N30.
     aKKp8u3Im_5dZKsgz6_1tMLx4K5sZ--rWHAgZ2F6fe0

182 *Journal of the Executive Proceedings of the Senate, Volume 38, Issue 2, Part*
     1. (United States: M. Glazier, Inc.) January 1, 1887) 376. https://books.
     google.com/books?id=VS8tAQAAMAAJ&pg=PA376&lpg=PA376&dq=Surgeo
     n+Lincoln+R.+Stone+Journal+of+the+U.S.+Senate+October+1865&source=
     bl&ots=UM9D1t2Wn-&sig=ACfU3U0nRsqiMElJMGbWGgsW6oc3D7UeVg&h
     l=en&sa=X&ved=2ahUKEwiFgtGV9YvqAhW2oHIEHUHLD1IQ6AEwAHoECA
     gQAQ#v=onepage&q=Surgeon%20Lincoln%20R.%20Stone%20Journal%20
     of%20the%20U.S.%20Senate%20October%201865&f=false Google Books.

183 "Massachusetts Death Index, 1901-1980, Volume Number 70," digi-
     tal images, Ancestry.com (https://www.ancestry.com/imageviewer/
     collections/3659/images/41263_2421406273_0069-00085?treeid=&
     personid=&hintid=&usePUB=true&_phsrc=OcA5109&_phstart=succe
     ssSource&usePUBJs=true&pId=2692960&backurl=https%3A%2F%2
     Fsearch.ancestry.com%2Fcgi-bin%2Fsse.dll%3Findiv%3D1%26dbid%
     3D3659%26h%3D2692960%26tid%3D%26pid%3D%26usePUB%3Dt

rue%26_phsrc%3DOcA5109%26_phstart%3DsuccessSource , accessed June 19, 2020) pg.504, entry for Lincoln Ripley Stone.

184 Theresa Kaminski, *Dr. Mary Walker's Civil War: One Woman's Journey to the Medal of Honor and the Fight for Women's Rights. (Lanham, Maryland: Lyons Press, 2020). 114. Accessed June 19, 2020.*

https://books.google.com/books?id=W-zSDwAAQBAJ&pg=PA114&lpg=PA1 14&dq=Civil+War+Surgeon+%22Francis+Salter%22&source=bl&ots=2miw-ObdLT&sig=ACfU3U22X2i7NlH3iR8D_UUXhkRd1e5rjA&hl=en&sa=X&ved= 2ahUKEwj_-MCL45DpAhUYH80KHb5hCSAQ6AEwDXoECAoQAQ#v=onepa ge&q=Civil%20War%20Surgeon%20%22Francis%20Salter%22&f=false Google Books.

185 *History of the campaign of the Cavalry Corps, Military Division of the Mississippi, in Alabama and Georgia from the 22nd of March to April 20, 1865.* http://www.aotc.net/selma-rep.htm#Wilson. Accessed February 6, 2020.

186 1870 U.S. Census, Pickaway County, Ohio, population schedule, Circleville, p. 36, dwelling 152, family 265, Mary Salter; digital image, Ancestry.com, accessed May 1, 2020.

https://www.ancestry.com/imageviewer/collections/7163/ images/4278455_00084?treeid=&personid=&hintid=&use PUB=true&_phsrc=OcA5117&_phstart=successSource&u sePUBJs=true&_ga=2.84039707.38735988.1592580124-407736261.1507342369&pId=40993290&backurl=https%3A%2F%2F search.ancestry.com%2Fcgi-bin%2Fsse.dll%3Findiv%3D1%26dbid%3 D7163%26h%3D40993290%26tid%3D%26pid%3D%26usePUB%3Dt rue%26_phsrc%3DOcA5117%26_phstart%3DsuccessSource

187 1870 U.S. Census, Washington, District of Columbia, p. 316, dwelling place 2185, family 2427, Francis and Eddie L. Salter; digital image, Ancestry. com, accessed May 1, 2020. https://www.ancestry.com/discoveryui-con-tent/view/2857239:7163?tid=&pid=&queryId=acab44f33db51730f05d7800 6bfd99f4&_phsrc=OcA7169&_phstart=successSource

188 Nicole Hixon, email to author, August 19, 2021.

189 Tennessee, U.S., Compiled Marriages, 1851-1900. https://www.ancestry. com/discoveryui-content/view/120399:4125?tid=&pid=&queryId=73f1673 5ced7319bf015df1b0bf8b205&_phsrc=OcA7171&_phstart=successSource Ancestry.com.

190 Washington, D.C., U.S., Select Deaths and Burials Index, 1769-1960. https://search.ancestry.com/cgi-bin/sse.dll?indiv=1&dbid=60260&h=376

390&tid=&pid=&queryId=73f16735ced7319bf015df1b0bf8b205&usePUB=t rue&_phsrc=OcA7173&_phstart=successSource Ancestry.com.

191 U.S. Find a Grave Index, 1600s-Current. https://www.findagrave.com/ memorial/11863310/mary-j-salter Findagrave.com via Ancestry.com.

192 1870 U.S. Census, Ohio, Clark County, Ohio, population schedule, Springfield, Ohio, p. 183, dwelling 4211, family 474, James and Sarah Bell; digital image, Ancestry.com, accessed June 19, 2020. https://search. ancestry.com/cgi-bin/sse.dll?indiv=1&dbid=7163&h=40567125&tid=&pid= &usePUB=true&_phsrc=OcA5125&_phstart=successSource

193 *Gallipolis Daily Tribune, July 24, 1899. Accessed April 2, 2020.* http:// bossardlibrary.advantage-preservation.com/viewer/?k=hannah%20 maxon%20springfield&i=f&by=1899&bdd=1890&d=07241899- 07241899&m=on&ord=k1&fn=gallipolis_daily_tribune_usa_ohio_gallipo- lis_18990724_english_1&df=1&dt=1 Bossard Library Digital Newspaper Archive.

194 1910 U.S. Census, Montgomery County, Ohio, population schedule, Dayton Ward 8, p.14, dwelling 28, family 162, Oscar V. and Mabel Bell; digital image, Ancestry.com, accessed June 20, 2020.

https://www.ancestry.com/imageviewer/collections/7884/images/4449 734_00955?pId=131293652&backurl=https%3A%2F%2Fwww.ancestry. com%2Ffamily-tree%2Fperson%2Ftree%2F25877486%2Fperson%2F18337 29511%2Ffacts%2Fcitation%2F5199479284%2Fedit%2Frecord

195 "U.S. National Homes for Disabled Volunteer Soldiers, 1866-1938," digital image, Ancestry.com, p.2652, accessed February 6, 2020, entry for James R. Bell. https://www.ancestry.com/imageviewer/collections/1200/images/ MIUSA1866_113765-00021?treeid=&personid=&hintid=&queryId=7bbcf5c9 522c565e8087d63dd980aa16&usePUB=true&_phsrc=OcA5127&_phstart=s uccessSource&usePUBJs=true&pId=487622&backurl=https%3A%2F%2Fs earch.ancestry.com%2Fcgi-bin%2Fsse.dll%3F_phsrc%3DOcA5127%26_phs tart%3DsuccessSource%26usePUBJs%3Dtrue%26indiv%3D1%26dbid%3D 1200%26gsfn%3DJames%26gsln%3DBell%26gsln_x%3D1%26gskw%3Ddo ctor%2C%2520physician%26msydy%3D1910%26msypn__ftp%3Ddayton% 2C%2520montgomery%2C%2520ohio%2C%2520usa%26msypn%3D52103 %26msbdy%3D1824%26msbpn__ftp%3Dpennsylvania%2C%2520usa%26 msbpn%3D41%26msrpn__ftp%3Dgallipolis%2C%2520gallia%2C%2520ohi o%2C%2520usa%26msrpn%3D51230%26new%3D1%26rank%3D1%26uid h%3Dueh%26redir%3Dfalse%26msT%3D1%26gss%3Dangs-d%26pcat%3D 39%26fh%3D0%26h%3D487622%26recoff%3D%26ml_rpos%3D1%26quer yId%3D7bbcf5c9522c565e8087d63dd980aa16

196 50th United States Congress, Report to accompany bill H.R. 3911, The Committee on Invalid Pensions, July 30, 1888. Congressional Serial Set.

197 1910 U.S. Census, Ringgold County, Iowa, population schedule, Tingley Town, p. 7, family no. 91, Charles C. and Sarah Bosworth; digital image, Ancestry.com, accessed February 6, 2020

https://www.ancestry.com/imageviewer/collections/7884/images/31111_4328312-01145?treeid=&personid=&hintid=&usePUB=true&_phsrc=OcA5129&_phstart=successSource&usePUBJs=true&_ga=2.21272377.38735988.1592580124-407736261.1507342369&pId=7569200&backurl=https%3A%2F%2Fsearch.ancestry.com%2Fcgi-bin%2Fsse.dll%3Findiv%3D1%26dbid%3D7884%26h%3D7569200%26tid%3D%26pid%3D%26usePUB%3Dtrue%26_phsrc%3DOcA5129%26_phstart%3DsuccessSource

198 1870 U.S. Census, Saline County, Missouri, population schedule, Grand Pass, p. 24, dwelling no. 164, family no. 172, Joseph R. and Agnes Lunbeck; digital image, Ancestry.com, accessed March 30, 2020

https://www.ancestry.com/imageviewer/collections/7163/images/4273849_00200?treeid=&personid=&hintid=&usePUB=true&_phsrc=OcA5131&_phstart=successSource&usePUBJs=true&_ga=2.115121029.38735988.1592580124-407736261.1507342369&pId=8820680&backurl=https%3A%2F%2Fsearch.ancestry.com%2Fcgi-bin%2Fsse.dll%3Findiv%3D1%26dbid%3D7163%26h%3D8820680%26tid%3D%26pid%3D%26usePUB%3Dtrue%26_phsrc%3DOcA5131%26_phstart%3DsuccessSource

199 Joseph R. Lunbeck and Agnes E. Truslow, grave marker, Grandview Cemetery, Chillicothe, Ross County, Ohio, digital image, s.v. "Joseph R. Lunbeck, Agnes E. Truslow. https://www.findagrave.com/memorial/117425751 Findagrave.com.

200 Ad, *Gallipolis Journal, June 24, 1869. Accessed January 22, 2020.* https://www.newspapers.com/image/70817670 Newspapers.com.

201 Ad, *Gallipolis Journal, August 25, 1870. Accessed January 22, 2020.* https://www.newspapers.com/image/83310878 Newspapers.com.

202 George Washington Livesay obituary, *Ironton Register, August 9, 1900. Thomas Livesay Lineage Page.*

203 "Riverby House," Ohio Memory Collection, image and description. Accessed June 17, 2020. https://www.ohiomemory.org/digital/collection/

p267401coll36/id/18956 Ohio History Connection website. French Art Colony website, http://www.frenchartcolony.org/

204 *The Dayton Herald, May 28, 1910. Obituary of Hannah Maxon. Accessed August 29, 2019*

https://www.newspapers.com/image/392816222 Newspapers.com.

205 "Your Home Town and Mine" column, *Gallipolis Daily Tribune, October 11, 1948. Accessed December 3, 2019*

http://bossardlibrary.advantage-preservation.com/ viewer/?k=hannah%20maxon&i=f&by=1948&bdd=1940&d=10111948-10111948&m=on&ord=k1&fn=gallipolis_daily_tribune_usa_ohio_gallipolis_19481011_english_2&df=1&dt=1 Bossard Library Digital Newspaper Archives.

206 Has Taught School for Forty Years: Three Generations Attended Reception Miss Maxon Gave in Honor of Her Pupils," *The Dayton Herald, June 14, 1902. Accessed August 29, 2019*

https://www.newspapers.com/image/394072382/?terms=Miss%2BMaxon

207 "Your Home Town and Mine" column, *Gallia Times, July 22, 1950. Accessed December 3, 2019.*

http://bossardlibrary.advantage-preservation.com/ viewer/?k=hannah%20maxon&i=f&by=1950&bdd=1950&d=01011950-12311950&m=between&ord=k1&fn=gallia_times_usa_ohio_gallipolis_19500722_english_4&df=1&dt=4 Bossard Library Digital Newspaper Archives.

208 Letter to the Editor, *Gallipolis Journal, August 20, 1874. Accessed August 28, 2019.*

https://www.newspapers.com/image/70790323/?terms=%22Hannah%2BMaxon%22%2Btemperance

209 "The Relief Corps: Gleanings from National Headquarters—Notes from Departments," *The National Tribune (Washington, D.C.), November 8, 1894. Accessed August 29, 2019.*

https://www.newspapers.com/image/46324796 Newspapers.com.

210 "Decoration Day: Duly Observed in Gallipolis. Graves Decorated and Able Addresses Delivered," *Gallipolis Daily Tribune, June 1, 1904. Accessed May 5, 2020.* http://bossardlibrary.advantage-preservation.com/ viewer/?k=decoration%20day&i=f&by=1904&bdd=1900&d=06011904-06011904&m=on&ord=k1&fn=gallipolis_daily_tribune_usa_ohio_gallipo-

lis_19040601_english_1&df=1&dt=1 Bossard Library Digital Newspaper Archives.

211 Anna E. Simmerman, "D.U.V. Has Three-Fold Interest in Pine Street Cemetery Memorial Day," *Gallipolis Daily Tribune, May 29, 1945. Accessed May 5, 2020.* http://bossardlibrary.advantage-preservation. com/viewer/?k=pine%20street&i=f&by=1945&bdd=1940&d=05291945-05291945&m=on&ord=k1&fn=gallipolis_daily_tribune_usa_ohio_gallipolis_19450529_english_4&df=1&dt=1 Bossard Library Digital Newspaper Archive.

212 "The Woman's Relief Corps: The 22nd National Convention a Dream of Delight—Boston's Hospitality Overpowering—Election of National Officers," *The National Tribune (Washington, D.C.), August 25, 1904. Accessed June 20, 2020.*

https://chroniclingamerica.loc.gov/data/batches/dlc_alicanto_ver02/data/sn82016187/00222252131/1904082501/0302.pdf *Chronicling America Digital Newspaper Archive, Library of Congress.*

213 Hannah U. Maxon, "The Relief Corps: Gleanings from National Headquarters—Notes from Departments," *The National Tribune (Washington, D.C.), May 9, 1895. Accessed August 29, 2019* https://www.newspapers.com/image/46186037/?terms=Maxon

214 "Hannah Maxon's Prayer: When News of the Assassination of President McKinley Came," *Gallipolis Daily Tribune, June 11, 1910. Accessed December 3, 2019.* http://bossardlibrary.advantage-preservation.com/viewer/?k=hannah%20maxon&i=f&by=1910&bdd=1910&d=06111910-06111910&m=on&ord=k1&fn=gallipolis_daily_tribune_usa_ohio_gallipolis_19100611_english_1&df=1&dt=1

215 *Journal of the Thirteenth Annual Convention of the Woman's Relief Corps, Auxiliary to the Grand Army of the Republic, Louisville, Kentucky, September 12th, 13th and 14th, 1895. (Boston, Massachusetts: E.B. Stillings & Co., 1895) 202-203.* https://books.google.com/books?id=HNgSAAAAYAAJ&pg=PA3&lpg=PA3&dq=Journal+of+the+Thirteenth+Annual+Convention+of+the+Woman%E2%80%99s+Relief+Corps,+Auxiliary+to+the+Grand+Army+of+the+Republic,+Louisville,+Kentucky,+September+12th,+13th+and+14th,+1895.&source=bl&ots=LstirQ54vw&sig=ACfU3U2u5D02SpDTeg_Xt5oRPZwym6Tt1w&hl=en&sa=X&ved=2ahUKEwi-m7K325rqAhX1mXIEHfRhCOwQ6AEwA3oECAkQAQ#v=onepage&q=Journal%20of%20the%20Thirteenth%20Annual%20Convention%20of%20the%20Woman%E2%80%99s%20Relief%20Corps%2C%20Auxiliary%20to%20the%20Grand%20Army%20of%20the%20Republic%2C%20

Louisville%2C%20Kentucky%2C%20September%2012th%2C%2013th%20 and%2014th%2C%201895.&f=false Google Books.

216 "Hannah Maxon Gets Pension: Draws $103.60 at July Disbursement in Columbus," *The Gallipolis Daily Tribune, August 6, 1907. Accessed December 3, 2019.* http://bossardlibrary.advantage-preservation.com/ viewer/?k=hannah%20maxon&i=f&by=1907&bdd=1900&d=08061907-08061907&m=on&ord=k1&fn=gallipolis_daily_tribune_usa_ohio_gallipo-lis_19070806_english_1&df=1&dt=1 Bossard Digital Newspaper Archives.

217 "Ohio Death Records, 1908-1932, 1938-2018," Hannah M. [sic] Maxon, digital image, from Ancestry.com. Accessed June 20, 2020.

https://www.ancestry.com/imageviewer/collections/5763/images/ ohvr_d_1908_1-2152?treeid=&personid=&hintid=&queryId=6329afdcb0eb7 713cc78a7efa05352da&usePUB=true&_phsrc=OcA5144&_phstart=success Source&usePUBJs=true&pId=6106231&backurl=https%3A%2F%2Fsearch. ancestry.com%2Fcgi-bin%2Fsse.dll%3F_phsrc%3DOcA5144%26_phstart% 3DsuccessSource%26usePUBJs%3Dtrue%26indiv%3D1%26dbid%3D5763 %26gsfn%3DHannah%2520U.%26gsln%3DMaxon%26cp%3D12%26gskw %3DTeacher%2C%2520nurse%2C%2520Civil%2520War%26_83004003-n_ xcl%3Dm%26msfng%3DSamuel%26msfns%3DMaxon%26msmng%3DEliz abeth%26msmns%3DRodgers%26msypn__ftp%3Dgallipolis%2C%2520galli a%2C%2520ohio%2C%2520usa%26msypn%3D51230%26msbdy%3D1841 %26msbdm%3D10%26msbpn__ftp%3Dgallipolis%2C%2520gallia%2C%25 20ohio%2C%2520usa%26msbpn%3D51230%26msddy%3D1910%26msdd m%3D5%26msddd%3D26%26msdpn__ftp%3Dgallipolis%2C%2520gallia% 2C%2520ohio%2C%2520usa%26msdpn%3D51230%26msrpn__ftp%3Dgall ia%2C%2520ohio%2C%2520usa%26msrpn%3D1109%26qh%3Dc0c28df61 509255f175dc507e0356901%26new%3D1%26rank%3D1%26uidh%3Dueh %26redir%3Dfalse%26gss%3Dangs-d%26pcat%3D34%26fh%3D0%26h%3 D6106231%26recoff%3D%26ml_rpos%3D1%26queryId%3D6329afdcb0eb7 713cc78a7efa05352da

218 "Ohio, Soldiers Grave Registration Cards, 1804-1958, Maxon, Hannah U., digital image, Fold3 (https://www.fold3.com/ image/615953040?xid=1022&_ga=2.84562843.38735988.1592580124-407736261.1507342369 , accessed December 3, 2019), pg. 1.

About the Author

Christy Perry Tuohey is an author and freelance writer. She was born and raised in West Virginia and is a graduate of Marshall University, Class of 1982.

She is a 30+ year veteran of newsrooms and classrooms. She was a TV news reporter and anchor in markets including Charleston/ Huntington, WV; Charlotte, NC; and Columbus and Cleveland, OH. Her writing has been published in multiple print and online newspapers and magazines including the *Cleveland Plain Dealer, Pillars Magazine, Family Times Magazine* and the *Charleston (WV) Gazette.* In the 2000s, Perry Tuohey taught journalism classes at the S.I. Newhouse School of Public Communications at Syracuse University.

You can find Christy on Facebook at https://www.facebook.com/CPTAuthor and https://www.facebook.com/panthermountain and on Twitter at https://twitter.com/CP2E

35th Star Publishing

Charleston, West Virginia

www.35thstar.com

Made in the USA
Monee, IL
02 July 2022